Legend

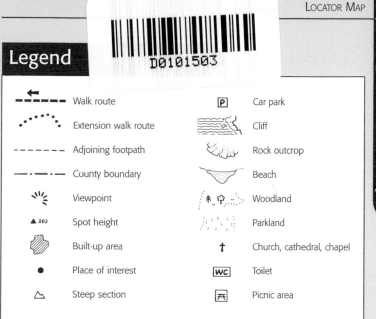

←-------	Walk route	P	Car park
••••••••	Extension walk route		Cliff
-------	Adjoining footpath		Rock outcrop
—•—•—•—	County boundary		Beach
☀	Viewpoint		Woodland
▲ 392	Spot height		Parkland
•	Built-up area		
•	Place of interest	†	Church, cathedral, chapel
△	Steep section	WC	Toilet
		⊼	Picnic area

Cornwall locator map

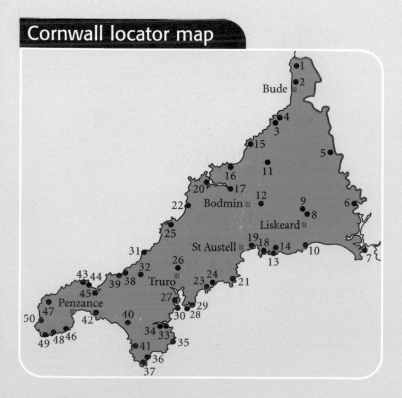

Contents

Contents

Rating: Each walk is rated for its relative difficulty compared to the other walks in this book. Walks marked 𝟐𝟐 𝟐𝟐 𝟐𝟐 are likely to be shorter and easier with little total ascent. The hardest walks are marked 𝟐𝟐 𝟐𝟐 𝟐𝟐 .

Walking in Safety: For advice and safety tips ➤ 128.

Introducing Cornwall

Cornwall's long, dwindling peninsula reaches out into the Atlantic like a ragged claw and nowhere in that peninsula is more than 20 miles (30km) from the sea. The Cornish coast is traversed by the Countryside Commission's 268 miles (431km) Cornwall Coast Path that runs like a neat parting through maritime heathland and coastal fields, along the edges of dramatic cliff-tops, and past magnificent beaches and picturesque fishing villages turned tourist resorts, such as Port Isaac, St Ives and Fowey. It is unsurprising, therefore, that Cornwall's extraordinary coastline is featured in a majority of the walking routes described in this book.

There is hardly any part of the Cornish coast that is not exhilarating. On the north coast you are made dramatically aware of the vagaries of the sea and of its interaction with the land. This is a world of stupendous cliffs, of deep inlets and wave-lashed promontories, a world where Atlantic swells roll across acres of golden sand and where you can see the weather changing a mile offshore. Yet, on windless summer days, the cliff tops are like fragrant gardens of wild flowers above a crystal clear sea. On Cornwall's south coast, the cliffs can be just as compelling, though they are less barren and rugged and are spared the worst of Atlantic storms. Here, the quieter waters of the English Channel breed less tumultuous seas, the land is lush and green, and coves and beaches have a captivating serenity.

In most cases coastal walks in Cornwall can be linked with inland paths, tracks and lanes to provide satisfying circular walks, often with typically Cornish country pubs, restaurants and cafés somewhere along the way. Many of the most picturesque stretches of the Cornish coast are in the care of the National Trust whose commitment to sensibly managed access has furnished numerous linking footpaths that enhance the pleasure of coastal walking. The work of Cornwall's County, District, and Parish councils, together with the co-operation of enlightened landowners and farmers, has seen a steady improvement in the upkeep of rights of way and in the development of permissive paths.

The coastline is a hard act to follow, but inland Cornwall also has much to offer the walker. On Bodmin Moor, and on the Land's End Peninsula, paths lead through haunting landscapes, punctuated by the stone circles and burial chambers of prehistoric cultures. The woods of Cardinham and Calstock feel so landlocked that you would think the sea was a thousand miles away.

PUBLIC TRANSPORT ⓘ

Cornwall is well served by public transport, but you need to plan carefully if tackling the linear walks, for which it is helpful to combine a car with public transport. The main bus company in Cornwall is First Western National. Information: East Cornwall (01752) 402060; Mid Cornwall (Walk 25) (01208) 79898; West Cornwall (Walks 40 and 50) (01209) 719988. Rail enquiries (Walks 10 and 45) (08457) 484950. For rail and bus information try the internet site www.pti.org.uk.

In Cornwall's towns and villages the distinctive character of this remarkable county is just as potent. Walk round Launceston, once the county town of an older Cornwall, and discover how much of its rich history is still reflected in the façades of old houses and in the medieval pattern of its streets. At Falmouth coast, enjoy the seagoing atmosphere of one of the world's biggest natural anchorages and one of Britain's most historic ports. At Polruan and Fowey, experience a palpable sense of how the sea, and a remote, secretive coastline, have shaped a colourful maritime past, when piracy and smuggling were an inescapable way of Cornish life.

All of Cornwall's vivid contrasts are emphasised when you travel on foot, far from busy highways and the predictable round of tourist attractions. In the 'First and Last' county in England, there is a fresh perspective round every corner, a unique sense of place everywhere you walk. Exploring Cornwall on foot is to experience the best that walking can offer in a landscape that is like nowhere else in Britain.

Using this Book

Information panels
An information panel for each walk shows its relative difficulty (➤ 5), the distance and total amount of ascent. An indication of the gradients you will encounter is shown by the rating ▲▲ ▲▲ ▲▲ (no steep slopes) to ▲▲ ▲▲ ▲▲ (several very steep slopes).

Maps
There are 30 maps, covering 40 of the walks. Some walks have a suggested option in the same area. The information panel for these walks will tell you how much extra walking is involved. On short-cut suggestions the panel will tell you the total distance if you set out from the start of the main walk. Where an option returns to the same point on the main walk, just the distance of the loop is given. Where an option leaves the main walk at one point and returns to it at another, then the distance shown is for the whole walk. The minimum time suggested is for reasonably fit walkers and doesn't allow for stops. Each walk has a suggested map. Laminated aqua3 maps are longer lasting and water resistant.

Start Points
The start of each walk is given as a six-figure grid reference prefixed by two letters indicating which 100km square of the National Grid it refers to. You'll find more information on grid references on most Ordnance Survey maps.

Dogs
We have tried to give dog owners useful advice about how dog friendly each walk is. Please respect other countryside users. Keep your dog under control, especially around livestock, and obey local bylaws and other dog control notices.

Car Parking
Many of the car parks suggested are public, but occasionally you may find you have to park on the roadside or in a lay-by. Please be considerate when you leave your car, ensuring that access roads or gates are not blocked and that other vehicles can pass safely.

The Vicar of Morwenstow's Gothic World

A walk through Cornwall's most northerly parish, one time home of the eccentric Victorian parson-poet, Robert Stephen Hawker.

•DISTANCE•	7 miles (11.3km)
•MINIMUM TIME•	4hrs
•ASCENT / GRADIENT•	1,640ft (500m) ▲▲▲
•LEVEL OF DIFFICULTY•	🏃 🏃 🏃
•PATHS•	Generally good, but inland paths and tracks can be very muddy during wet weather
•LANDSCAPE•	High cliffs punctuated by deep grassy valleys and backed by quiet woods and farmland
•SUGGESTED MAP•	aqua3 OS Explorer 126 Clovelly & Hartland
•START / FINISH•	Grid reference: SS 206154
•DOG FRIENDLINESS•	Dogs off lead in places, but under strict control in fields and grazed cliffland
•PARKING•	Morwenstow: Follow signposted road from the A39 about 2½ miles (4.4km) north of Kilkhampton. Small free car park by Morwenstow Church and Rectory Farm Tearooms
•PUBLIC TOILETS•	Duckpool

BACKGROUND TO THE WALK

The Gothic landscape of North Cornwall's Morwenstow parish, all gaunt sea cliffs, backed by remote farmland and wonderfully gloomy woods, was the ideal environment for the 19th-century parson-poet the Reverend Robert Stephen Hawker. Hawker was vicar of the parish from 1834 to 1874. He was devoted to his parishioners, most of whom were poor farmers and labourers. He cared also for the victims of shipwrecks on the savage Morwenstow coast. There were few survivors, but Hawker made it his duty to bury the dead. He would search the barely accessible foreshore beneath the cliffs, dressed in sea boots and a fisherman's smock, and salvage the often gruesome remains. Legend says that the vicar often dosed his reluctant helpers with gin to overcome their revulsion and superstition. The graveyard at Morwenstow pays homage to the drowned of numerous wrecks.

Hawker is said to have dosed himself with other substances too. He smoked opium, in keeping with the habits of fashionable Romantic poets such as Coleridge and de Quincy. At the tiny 'Hawker's Hut', a driftwood shack that nestles just below the cliff top near the beginning of this walk, he wrote and meditated, often under the influence. He is said to have dressed as a mermaid on occasions, took his pet pig, Gyp, for long walks, and once excommunicated a cat for catching a mouse on Sunday. And why not?

Dramatic Landscape

Take the spirits of Parson Hawker and Gyp the pig with you through this dramatic landscape as you walk from the splendid Church of St Morwenna out to the edge of the great cliffs, to Hawker's Hut. From here the coast path dips into and out of dramatic valleys, often

Walk 1

within sight of the slate-grey fins of smooth slabby rock that protrude from the cliff edge. The route leads past the Government's eerie radio tracking station at Cleve where huge satellite receivers cup their ears to the sky.

At Duckpool, the cliffs relent and you turn inland and away from the often boisterous coast to find picturesque thatched cottages beside a placid river ford. Beyond lies the calm of deep woodland. Yet there lingers even here, a sense of Morwenstow's other-worldliness, as the route winds through lonely fields and past handsome old manor houses at Eastaway, Stanbury and Tonacombe to reach Morwenstow's welcoming pub and then Parson Hawker's handsome church once more.

Walk 1 Directions

① Follow the signposted track from the car park to the coast path, then turn left. You'll reach **Hawker's Hut** in about 100yds (91m). Continue from here along the coast path to **Duckpool**.

② When you reach the inlet of Duckpool walk up the road along the bottom of the valley to a T-junction and turn left. At a junction, go right to cross a bridge beside a ford. Follow the lane round left for about 150yds (137m), then bear off left along a broad track through some woodland.

③ Cross a stile on the left, go over a wooden footbridge, climb the slope, then turn right and up a track. Turn left at a T-junction, keep ahead at the next junction, then in 40yds (37m) go right through a metal gate.

④ Follow a field track leading to a surfaced lane at **Woodford**. Turn left and go downhill past **Shears Farm** then round right and uphill to a junction with a road. Turn left past a **bus shelter**.

> ### WHAT TO LOOK FOR ⓘ
> Parson Hawker's eccentricity extended to the vicarage he built next to Morwenstow church. The house's chimneys replicate the towers of other North Cornwall churches and the tower of an Oxford college. The kitchen chimney is a replica of the tombstone of Hawker's mother.

⑤ Turn left along a path between cottages to a kissing gate. Turn right and then immediately left and follow the edge of the field to a stile on the left. Cross this stile, then cross the next field, bearing slightly left, to reach the hedge on the opposite side.

⑥ Go over two stiles and then straight up the next field, often muddy, to a hedge corner. Go alongside a wall to a hedged track and on to a junction with a surfaced lane.

⑦ Go through a gate opposite, then turn right through a gap. Go left to a stile. Bear left across the next field to its far left-hand corner, then go up to **Stanbury House**. Turn right to reach a surfaced lane.

> ### WHILE YOU'RE THERE ⓘ
> Morwenstow's **Church of St Morwenna** is unavoidable and unmissable, from its atmospheric graveyard and splendid Norman doorways to its wonderfully gloomy interior. Even the approach to the lychgate has drama. You tread on visible depressions, bare of pebbles, the graves of unsanctified suicides or criminals. Just inside the gate, on the right is a granite cross with the initials of Hawker's wife. The cross on the left commemorates drowned sailors.

⑧ Go left along the lane for a few paces and then over a narrow stile on the right. Go straight across the next two fields to reach a stile and gate into a farm lane behind **Tonacombe House**.

⑨ Go right for a few paces then bear off left along a muddy track. Cross two fields then descend into a wooded valley. Keep right, cross a stream, then go right and up steeply to a stile.

⑩ Cross over the fields to reach a meadow behind the **Bush Inn**. Go down the left side of the buildings, and then up to the road. Turn left for **Morwenstow Church** and the car park.

> ### WHERE TO EAT AND DRINK ⓘ
> There are no refreshments along the way but the **Bush Inn** is just along the road from Morwenstow Church. It does bar meals and you can enjoy smoked mackerel or crab salad with your Hick's Special Draught. The delightful **Rectory Farm Tearooms & Restaurant** is right at the start of the walk and offers morning coffee, lunches, cream teas and evening meals by arrangement.

A Wild Flower Fiesta at Bude

A pleasant stroll through coastal heathland where the cliff edges provide a refuge for masses of wild flowers.

•DISTANCE•	5 miles (8km)
•MINIMUM TIME•	2hrs 30min
•ASCENT / GRADIENT•	262ft (80m)
•LEVEL OF DIFFICULTY•	
•PATHS•	Excellent throughout. The National Trust is carrying out regeneration of some eroded sections; please heed notices
•LANDSCAPE•	Coastal cliffs. Keep well back from the cliff edges
•SUGGESTED MAP•	aqua3 OS Explorer 111 Bude, Boscastle & Tintagel and 126 Clovelly & Hartland
•START / FINISH•	Grid reference: SS 204071
•DOG FRIENDLINESS•	Dogs on lead through grazed areas
•PARKING•	Crooklets Beach Car Park. Follow signs for Crooklets. Large pay-and-display car park, can be very busy in summer
•PUBLIC TOILETS•	Crooklets Beach and Sandy Mouth

BACKGROUND TO THE WALK

The windswept coastal grasslands of North Cornwall seem unlikely havens for plant life, but, around the seaside resort of Bude, the cliff edges especially, provide a unique refuge for fascinating wild flowers. This walk follows the flat cliff land north of Bude with an inland section on the return. Along the way you'll find numerous wild flowers that turn the cliff top into a riot of colour in spring and early summer.

Grasslands

The walk starts from the northern outskirts of Bude at Crooklets Beach and within minutes takes you out onto the cropped grasslands of the National Trust's Maer Cliff and Maer Down. In spring the dominant flower here is the spring squill, whose distinctive powder-blue flowers are dotted across the grass. Other early plants which flourish here are the lilac-coloured early scurvy grass, the pink thrift and white sea-campion. At Northcott Mouth the cliffs give way to a wide stony beach. Here the route of the walk turns inland and climbs steadily uphill to eventually follow the line of an old bridleway, often choked with a tangle of grass and brambles, but with typical hedgrow plants such as foxglove and red valerian poking through.

Yellow Heads

Soon you reach the road to Sandy Mouth Beach and the cliff path back to Crooklets. Once more there are many wild flowers here. The grass is laced with the yellow and orange flowers of kidney vetch and the yellow heads of hawkweed and, by July, is scattered with the pink and white florets of the aromatic wild carrot. From Crooklets the walk angles inland to a final stroll through an area of typically dense woodland, a dramatic contrast in habitat to the open cliff top. Here primroses and daffodils appear, brightening up the early spring. A mixture of trees such as sycamore, beech, alder, cypress, Scots pine and Corsican pine create a sheltered and moist environment within which plants like the tall yellow flag iris and the lilac-coloured water mint thrive. The last section of the walk leads you past the Maer Lake Nature Reserve, a large area of wetland, that is flooded in winter and is in the care of the Cornwall Wildlife Trust and the Cornwall Birdwatching and Preservation Society. There is no public access to the area from the roadside but you can get an excellent view of the many birds through binoculars.

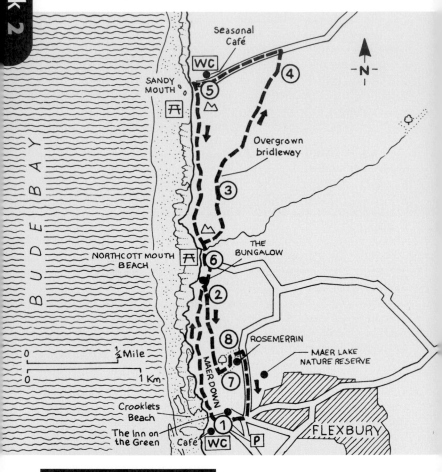

Walk 2 Directions

① Go towards the beach, cross a bridge and head for some steps. Pass in front of beach huts, then turn left along a stony track between walls. Go up some steps and onto the coast path, signposted 'Maer Cliff.

② Go through a gate and along a track behind a white building, called the **Bungalow**. Bear off to the left, by a signpost, down a path to the sea at **Northcott Mouth beach**. From here, bear right along a track that will take you back inland, past a group of houses on the left, and continue uphill to pass some more houses.

WHERE TO EAT AND DRINK ⓘ
There is a **National Trust seasonal café** in an attractive building above Sandy Mouth Beach at the halfway point of the walk. Snacks, teas and ice creams are available. There are a number of beachside cafés at Crooklets Beach. Just across the road from the car park entrance at the start of the walk, the **Inn On The Green** does good pub lunches.

WHAT TO LOOK FOR ⓘ
Butterflies that are likely to be seen along the cliffs in summer include the meadow brown, probably Britain's commonest butterfly, its name a perfect description of its dusky colour. Look also for the common blue, a small butterfly with an almost lilac tinge, and for the glamorous painted lady with its tawny-orange wings and black and white markings. The painted lady's main habitat is Southern Spain and North Africa from where large swarms often migrate north in April and May, finding no difficulty in crossings of the English Channel.

③ Where the track bends round to the right, leave it and keep straight ahead to a gate. Keep outside the left edge of the overgrown bridle path ahead.

④ Reach a field gate and follow a track through fields. Keep left at a junction with another track, then continue to a T-junction with a public road. Turn left and walk down the road, with care, to **Sandy Mouth**.

⑤ Pass the **National Trust information kiosk** and descend towards the beach, then go left and uphill and follow the coast path back to **Northcott Mouth beach**, and a red lifeguard hut passed earlier.

⑥ Follow the roadside path just past the lifeguard hut and retrace your steps to the white Bungalow passed earlier. Go along the track behind the building and then keep ahead along a broad track with a field hedge on your left.

⑦ At a field corner by a footpath sign go through the gate ahead then turn left and follow the field edge into a hedged-in path. Continue between trees to a lane by a house at **Rosemerrin**. Continue to a road.

⑧ Turn right along the road, with **Maer Lake Nature Reserve** down to your left. Cross at a junction with **Maer Down Road**, go left, then right, and return to the **car park**.

Walk 3

The Dramatic Geology of Crackington Haven

A coastal and inland walk with views of the spectacular sea cliffs of the North Cornish coast.

•DISTANCE•	3½ miles (5.7km)
•MINIMUM TIME•	1hr 45min
•ASCENT / GRADIENT•	270ft (82m)
•LEVEL OF DIFFICULTY•	
•PATHS•	Good coastal footpath and woodland tracks. Can be very wet and muddy
•LANDSCAPE•	Open coast and wooded valley
•SUGGESTED MAP•	aqua3 OS Explorer 111, Bude, Boscastle & Tintagel
•START / FINISH•	Grid reference: SX 145969
•DOG FRIENDLINESS•	Dogs on lead through grazed areas
•PARKING•	Crackington Haven car park. From the A39 at Wainhouse Corner, or from Boscastle on the B3263. Can be busy in summer. Burden Trust car park, along B3263 road to Wainhouse
•PUBLIC TOILETS•	Crackington Haven

BACKGROUND TO THE WALK

Crackington Haven has given its name to a geological phenomena, the Crackington Formation, a fractured shale that has been shaped into incredibly twisted and contorted forms. On the sheared-off cliff faces of the area, you can see the great swirls and folds of this sedimentary rock that was 'metamorphosised' by volcanic heat and contorted by the geological storms of millions of years ago. Even the name Crackington derives from the Cornish word for sandstone, *crak*. The very sound, in English, hints at friability and dramatic decay. Scripted across the face of the vast cliffs traversed by this walk are the anticlines, (upward folds) and synclines (downward folds) that are so characteristic of these great earth movements.

A Small Port

During the 18th and 19th centuries, Crackington Haven was a small port, landing coal and limestone and shipping out local agricultural produce and slate. Small coastal ships would anchor off the beach, or settle on the sands at low tide, in order to exchange cargoes. Plans to expand Crackington into a major port were made in the early 19th century. The grandiose scheme aimed to build huge breakwaters to protect Crackington and the neighbouring Tremoutha Haven from the, often huge, Atlantic swells. Quays and docks were to be built inside the protected harbour. A rail link to Launceston was proposed and a small new town planned for the Haven, which was to be renamed Port Victoria.

As with many development plans of the time, the scheme did not materialise, otherwise the Crackington Haven of today might have been a dramatically different place. As you set out along the open cliff south from Crackington, the remarkable nature of the geology unfolds. Looking back from Bray's Point, you see clearly the massive contortions in the high cliff face of Pencannow Point on the north side of Crackington. Soon the path leads above Tremoutha Haven and up to the cliff edge beyond the domed headland of Cambeak. From here there is a breathtaking view of the folded strata and quartzite bands of Cambeak's cliffs. A path leads out to the tip of the headland, but it is precarious and is not recommended especially if it is wet or windy. The geology of the cliffs is still active, and, one day, erosion will destroy the neck of the headland, transforming Cambeak into an island, but preferably without you on it.

A short distance further on you arrive above Strangles Beach where again you look back to such fantastic features as Northern Door, a promontory of harder rock pierced by a natural arch where softer shales have been eroded by the sea. Where the route of the walk turns inland there is a line of low cliffs set back from the main cliff edge. These represent the old wounds of a land slip where the cliff has slumped towards the sea. From here the second part of the walk turns inland and descends into East Wood and the peaceful Trevigue Valley, itself part of a great geological extravaganza having once been a 'fiord' filled by the sea. Today much of the valley is a nature reserve and wandering down its leafy length is a splendid antidote to the coastal drama of the Crackington cliffs.

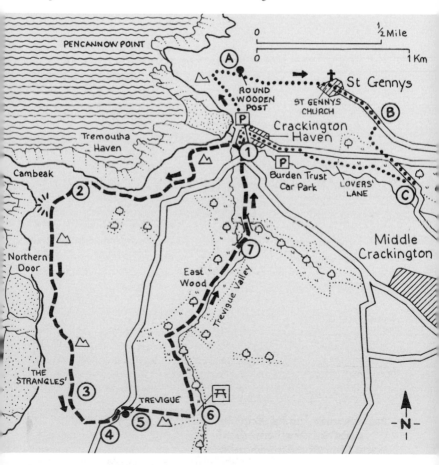

Walk 3

Walk 3 Directions

① From the **Crackington Haven** car park entrance go left across a bridge, then turn right at a **telephone kiosk**. Follow a broad track round to the left, between a signpost and an old wooden seat, then go through a kissing gate onto the coast path.

WHILE YOU'RE THERE
At Point ③, where the route turns inland, you can continue along the coast path for a few paces to where a path leads down right to a stile, from where another path leads down to **The Strangles beach**. Until well into the 20th century such beaches were a source of seaweed and sand for use as fertiliser on local fields. The track down to the beach gave access for donkeys. A visit to the beach is worthwhile, in spite of the steep return. You can view the remarkable coastal features from sea level.

② Keep left and follow a path up a sheltered valley on the inland side of the steep hill, then continue on the cliff path.

③ Where a stretch of low inland cliffs begins, just beyond a signpost and a few paces before a second signpost, go left along a path to reach a road by a National Trust sign for 'The Strangles'.

④ Go left, walking past the farm entrance to **Trevigue**, then, in just a few paces, turn right down a drive by the Trevigue sign. Then bear off to the left across the grass to go through a gate by a signpost.

⑤ Go directly down the field, keeping left of a telegraph pole, to reach a stile. Continue downhill to the edge of a wood. Go down a tree-shaded path to a junction of paths in a shady dell by the river.

⑥ Turn sharp left here, following the signpost towards **Haven**, and continue on the obvious path down the wooded river valley.

⑦ Cross a footbridge, then turn left at a junction with a track. Cross another footbridge and continue to a gate by some houses. Follow a track and then a surfaced lane to the main road, then turn left to the **car park.**

WHAT TO LOOK FOR   ⓘ
The field and woodland section of this walk supports a very different flora to that found on the heathery, windswept cliffland. Some of the most profuse field edge and woodland plants belong to the carrot family, the *Umbelliferae*. They may seem hard to distinguish, but the commonest is cow parsley, identifiable by its reddish stalk, feathery leaves and clustered white flower heads. Hogweed is a much larger umbellifer often standing head and shoulders above surrounding plants; it has hairy stalks and broad toothed leaves and can cause an unpleasant rash if it comes in contact with your skin. A third common umbellifer is the alexander, prolific in spring and early summer. It has broad, lime green leaves and clustered yellow florets.

Along the Cliffs to the Church of St Genny

There is still more to see at Crackington if you follow this little extension.
See map and information panel for Walk 3

Walk 4

•DISTANCE•	2½ miles (4km) for this extra loop
•MINIMUM TIME•	1hr 15min
•ASCENT / GRADIENT•	440ft (134m) ▲▲▲
•LEVEL OF DIFFICULTY•	🚶🚶 🚶 🚶

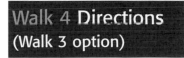

Walk 4 Directions (Walk 3 option)

On returning to **Crackington** and Point ①, from Walk 3, go up the road behind the pub for about 100yds (91m). Look out on the left for a coast path signpost, and a signpost to **St Genny's Church** beside a thatched cottage. From here the path rises unrelentingly to the top of the towering **Pencannow Point**. Take your time and the climb is surprisingly easy; there is a welcome seat at the top.

You are now perched above the awesome cliff seen from Walk 3 at Point ②. Pencannow is merely the root of a much higher land mass, worn down by millions of years of erosion. For the airiest of views you can follow a precarious path out along the narrow headland itself, but take care, especially when it is wet under foot or there are strong winds blowing.

On the main route, follow the coast path sharply round to the right and then along the cliff edge to reach a

kissing gate onto open ground. Beyond the gate head inland past a round wooden post, Point Ⓐ, to reach a kissing gate into a field. Follow the left-hand field edge to reach **St Genny's Church**. The tiny settlement of St Genny's is crouched in a protective fold of the coastal hills. The church of the same name is a sturdy little building with traceable Norman origins.

> **WHERE TO EAT AND DRINK** ⓘ
> The **Coombe Barton Inn** at Crackington Haven has spacious bars, a children's room and a good selection of food and drink. There are also two cafés to either side of the car park entrance.

Coming back up from the church, turn left and follow the lane, then go right at the first junction, Point Ⓑ. Descend steeply to reach the main road. Cross it with care and continue downhill. Go over a stone stile on the right, Point Ⓒ, signposted to **Crackington Haven**, and onto a woodland path. This is the beginning of '**Lovers' Lane**' a path that wends its romantic way along leafy tracks and above river meadows to reach the main road into **Crackington Haven**.

Walk 5

A Stroll through Historic Launceston

Exploring the fascinating streets and the surrounding countryside of Cornwall's ancient county town.

•DISTANCE•	2 miles (3.2km)
•MINIMUM TIME•	3hrs
•ASCENT / GRADIENT•	131ft (40m) ▲ ▲ ▲
•LEVEL OF DIFFICULTY•	🚶 🚶 🚶
•PATHS•	Paved walkways and field paths
•LANDSCAPE•	Townscape and grassy river valley
•SUGGESTED MAP•	Launceston Town Map
•START / FINISH•	Grid reference: SX 332845
•DOG FRIENDLINESS•	Dogs on lead through fields
•PARKING•	Number of car parks in Launceston
•PUBLIC TOILETS•	Walk House car park

Walk 5 Directions

Launceston was the chief town of Cornwall during medieval times. The high hill at the heart of the town was probably fortified as early as the Bronze Age, but today, the striking remains of a Norman castle survive and dominate the surrounding scene. There was an important monastic settlement here also and as late as the 1830s, Launceston was still Cornwall's county town. The legacy of all this is one of the most intriguing townscapes in the county.

Start your walk in the **Town Square** whose fine buildings include the Georgian **White Hart Hotel** with its 12th-century doorway, said to have been plundered many years ago from the ruins of **St Thomas's Priory**. Leave the Square by its north side and go down **High Street**. On the right-hand corner are the slightly leaning medieval

façades of Nos 11 and 13, slate-hung and painted cream, and with an overhung third storey. At the bottom of High Street turn right along **Church Street**, then cross over into **Southgate Street**, passing a number of fine buildings as you go. Part way down, on the right, is **Ching's Alley**, the name celebrating

> ### WHILE YOU'RE THERE ⓘ
> Make sure to visit the 16th-century **Church of St Mary Magdalene**, a remarkable building, not least for the wealth of carving on its generally unmanageable granite stonework. Inside the church is a famous recumbent statue of Mary Magdalene. An enduring local belief is that if you toss a pebble over your shoulder and it lands in the hollow of her back, then good fortune will follow. The **Lawrence House Museum** in Castle Street has a fascinating collection of memorabilia and artefacts that tell the story of the town from earliest times. **Launceston Castle** is an outstanding example of Norman fortification and there is an exhibition that tells the history of the site.

WHAT TO LOOK FOR ℹ

The history of towns and villages is often written across the upper storeys of their buildings. Take time to study façades, especially in the main streets of Launceston. Look for the painted pheonix at **No 4 High Street**, the old sign for a chemists. Look for the lute player and the angel opposite. At the corner of High Street and Church Street admire the twisted columns and elliptical windows of **No 20** and look for '**Hayman's Pianoforte Warehouse**' in Church Street.

a family of 19th-century wine and spirit merchants. An information board, just inside the alley, records some fascinating tales. At the bottom of Southgate Street is one of Launceston's glories, **Southgate Arch**, a sole survivor of the old town gateways.

From the **Southgate Street** side of the arch go left down the alleyway of **Blindhole**, then bear round left and past the old market on the left. Ahead lies one of Launceston's finest buildings, the **Church of St Mary Magdalene**, (► While You're There). Follow **Northgate Street** as it curves left and downhill into **Castle Street**. At the bottom of the hill, on the left, is the elegant **Eagle House**, now a hotel and one of Castle Street's fine row of Georgian houses. Bear right to **Lawrence House**, owned by the National Trust and containing Launceston's museum (► While You're There). A few paces further down the street, go down some steps on the left, past a row of old cottages and the **Northgate Inn**, to reach the bottom of **Tower Street**. Cross **Dockacre Hill** and go down **St Thomas Hill**, then turn left at the bottom and cross the busy main road with great care. Turn right, pass the post office, then turn left along

Riverside. The river is spanned here by an old packhorse bridge known as **Prior's Bridge**. On the left is the **Church of St Thomas**; behind this lie the impressive, but rather forlorn, ruins of the 12th-century Augustinian **Priory of St Thomas**.

Continue along Riverside and, on the right and just beyond the bridge, look for a plaque celebrating Launceston's great literary son, the poet Charles Causley. Keep walking on past a bowling green, cross a bridge over the **Launceston Steam Railway**, then turn left at a T-junction. Go past a row of cottages, then, at the corner of **Tredydan Road**, keep straight ahead along a surfaced track and on into a lane. Continue into **Wood Lane**, then at a bend just past a row of cottages, go right and over a stile. Follow a path for about ½ mile (800m), over stiles and through fields below **Launceston Castle**, to reach a road. Turn left and uphill to join **Western Road** and continue to the busy junction with **St Thomas Road**. On the right is the handsome Gothic **Guildhall** with its wooden Black Jacks that strike a quarterly bell. Opposite is the entrance to the town's ultimate glory, its Norman castle. Continue up **Western Road** to the **Town Square**.

WHERE TO EAT AND DRINK ℹ

The **White Hart Hotel** in Launceston's Town Square has large and comfortable bars and offers a good selection of bar meals. Just next to the Church of St Mary Magdalene in Tower Street is the long established **Bell Inn** where you can also get bar meals. Alongside Southgate Arch is the licensed bistro-restaurant **Three Steps to Heaven** serving excellent breakfasts, lunches and evening meals. There are a number of other cafés and restaurants around the town centre.

Tudor Cotehele and Victorian Calstock

A stroll along the River Tamar from Calstock's Victorian viaduct to the Tudor manor house of Cotehele.

•DISTANCE•	4 miles (6.4km)
•MINIMUM TIME•	3hrs
•ASCENT / GRADIENT•	164ft (50m) ▲ ▲ ▲
•LEVEL OF DIFFICULTY•	秌 秌 秌
•PATHS•	Excellent woodland tracks, can be muddy in places
•LANDSCAPE•	Wooded riverside
•SUGGESTED MAP•	aqua3 OS Explorer 108 Lower Tamar Valley & Plymouth
•START / FINISH•	Grid reference: SX 436683
•DOG FRIENDLINESS•	Dogs should be kept under control in Cotehele environs
•PARKING•	Calstock Quay car park. Bear right at junction at bottom of steep descent into the village. Free car park, but limited spaces. Often full by mid-morning
•PUBLIC TOILETS•	Calstock Quay, Cotehele House, Cotehele Quay

BACKGROUND TO THE WALK

The River Tamar seems to take its ease at Calstock and Cotehele, where it coils lazily through the lush countryside of the Devon-Cornwall border. Today all is rural peace and quiet. Yet a century ago Calstock was a bustling river port, and had been since Saxon times. Victorian copper and tin mining turned Calstock into an even busier port at which all manner of trades developed, including shipbuilding.

The coming of the railway brought an end to Calstock's importance. The mighty rail viaduct of 1906 that spans the river here is an enduring memorial to progress and to later decline, yet the Calstock of today retains the compact charm of its steep riverside location. The viaduct was built from specially cast concrete blocks – 11,000 of them were made on the Devon shore – and it is a tribute to its design that such thoroughly industrial architecture should seem so elegant today and should have become such an acceptable element in the Tamar scene.

Cotehele

The area's finest architectural gem is the Tudor manor house of Cotehele, the focus of this walk. Cotehele dates mainly from the late 15th and early 16th centuries. In the 17th century the Edgcumbe family, who owned the estate, transferred their seat to Mount Edgcumbe House overlooking Plymouth Sound (▶ Walk 7). Cotehele ceased to be the family's main home and the house was spared too much overt modernisation. Soon the Edgcumbe's came to appreciate the value of the house's Tudor integrity and Cotehele seems to have been preserved for its own sake, from the 18th century onwards.

The Edgcumbe's gave the house to the National Trust in 1947 and Cotehele survives as one of the finest Tudor buildings in England. The medieval plan of the house is intact; the fascinating complex of rooms, unlit by artificial light, creates an authentic atmosphere that transcends any suggestion of 'theme park' history. This is a real insight into how wealthier people lived in Tudor Cornwall. Cotehele was built with privacy and even defence in mind and the materials used are splendidly rustic; the exterior facades have a rough patina that adds to the authenticity.

The Danescombe Valley

The early part of the walk leads beneath an arch of the Calstock Viaduct and on along the banks of the river, past residential properties where busy quays and shipbuilding yards once stood. Most of the walk leads through the deeply wooded Danescombe Valley, whose trees crowd round Cotehele in a seamless merging with the splendid estate gardens. The gardens support azaleas and rhododendrons and a profusion of broadleaf trees, the whole interspersed with terraces and such charming features as a lily pond, a medieval dovecote and a Victorian summerhouse. Below the house, at Cotehele Quay, the preserved sailing barge, the *Shamrock*, and the National Maritime Museum's exhibition rooms, commemorate the great days of Tamar trade. As you walk back to Calstock, along an old carriageway and through the deeper recesses of the Danescombe Valley, it is easy to imagine the remote, yet vibrant life of this once great estate and of the busy river that gave it substance.

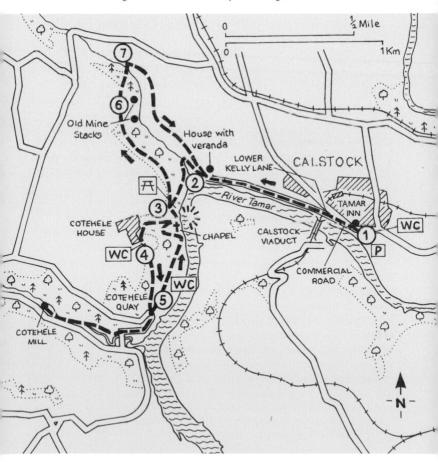

Walk 6

Walk 6 Directions

① From the car park walk to the left of the **Tamar Inn**, then turn left into **Commercial Road**. In a few paces take the second turning left and go along **Lower Kelly Lane** and beneath **Calstock Viaduct**.

② Keep left at a fork just past the large house with a veranda. Beyond a row of cottages, branch left, signposted '**Cotehele House**', and follow a broad track uphill and beneath trees.

WHERE TO EAT AND DRINK

The **Barn Restaurant** is an elegant National Trust restaurant within the Cotehele House complex. It serves morning coffee, afternoon tea and meals using much local produce and has a fine wine list. The **Edgcumbe Arms Tea Room** is an attractive small restaurant at Cotehele Quay offering similar fare to the Barn Restaurant. The **Tamar Inn** at Calstock Quay is right by the start of the walk and is a traditional pub serving a range of bar meals.

③ Go right at a junction, signposted '**Cotehele House**'. Pass above a dovecote in **Cotehele Gardens**, then turn left at a T-junction. Go through a gate and turn right for the entrance to Cotehele House.

④ Follow the road from **Cotehele House**, then branch left and downhill to reach **Cotehele Quay**.

(You can continue from the Quay for just under ½ mile (800m) to visit **Cotehele Mill**.)

WHILE YOU'RE THERE

Visit the outstation of the **National Maritime Museum** at Cotehele Quay where the story of Tamar River trade throughout the centuries is told in old pictures and displays. **Cotehele Quay Gallery** has exhibitions of painting and is located by the quay car park. **Cotehele Mill** lies a short distance (signposted) from Cotehele Quay and has been restored to working order.

⑤ Follow a path that starts beside the car park and just beyond **Cotehele Quay Gallery**. Pass a little chapel and then a superb viewpoint to Calstock. At a junction, go right, signposted **Calstock**. In a few paces branch left up a rising track.

⑥ Go right at a junction and descend to a wooden footbridge over a stream. At a T-junction with another track, turn left and walk up the track for about 55 yds (50m).

⑦ Turn sharply right and go up a rising track along the side of a stone wall. Pass a stone pillar and an old well on your left, then pass a junction with a track coming in from the left.

⑧ Join the surfaced lane just before the big house with a veranda, passed earlier. Retrace your steps to **Calstock Quay**.

WHAT TO LOOK FOR

The deep oak and beech woods that cloak the Danescombe Valley and Cotehele are a haven to wild life. The otter, an endangered species, may still be found along the Tamar's banks and although you would be immensely lucky to spot one, keep your eyes peeled. Buzzards lord it above clearings in the trees and above the neighbouring meadows. Along the minor streams, kingfishers patrol their territory, although again you need to keep a sharp lookout for them. In spring and early summer, the woods and meadows round Cotehele are thick with daffodils and bluebells.

The Cornish Shores of Plymouth Sound

A walk round the Mount Edgcumbe estate on the shores of Plymouth Sound.

•DISTANCE•	8 miles (12.9km)
•MINIMUM TIME•	4hrs
•ASCENT / GRADIENT•	328ft (100m) ▲▲▲
•LEVEL OF DIFFICULTY•	🚶 🚶 🚶
•PATHS•	Good throughout. Muddy in places in wet weather, 8 stiles
•LANDSCAPE•	Wooded shoreline of tidal creek, fields, woods and coast
•SUGGESTED MAP•	aqua3 OS Explorer 108 Lower Tamar Valley & Plymouth
•START / FINISH•	Grid reference: SX 453534
•DOG FRIENDLINESS•	Dogs on lead through grazed areas
•PARKING•	Cremyll car park. Alternatively reach Cremyll by ferry from the Plymouth side. Daily service between Admiral's Hard, Stonehouse, Plymouth and Cremyll
•PUBLIC TOILETS•	Cremyll and Kingsand

BACKGROUND TO THE WALK

The Mount Edgcumbe Country Park is a green oasis that flies in the face of Plymouth's crowded waterfront opposite. The two are separated by The Narrows, a few hundred yards (metres) of the 'Hamoaze', the estuary formed by the rivers Tavy, Lynher and Tamar. Mount Edgcumbe stands on the Cornish side of the river, although it was not always 'Cornish'. In Anglo Saxon times, Devon extended across the estuary as far as Kingsand, the halfway point in this walk. Today, however, Mount Edgcumbe and its waterfront settlement of Cremyll are emphatically Cornish. They stand on the most easterly extension of the Rame Peninsula, known with ironic pride by local people as the 'Forgotten Corner'. In truth Rame is one of the loveliest parts of the South West, let alone of Cornwall, and this walk takes you round the shores of the inner estuary, and then over the spine of the eastern peninsula to Kingsand, before returning to Cremyll along the open shores of Plymouth Sound.

Empacombe

The first section of the route takes you to peaceful Empacombe, where there is a tiny harbour contained within a crescent-shaped quay. It was here, during 1706–9, that workshops servicing the building of the famous Eddystone Lighthouse were located. Behind the harbour is the Gothic facade of Empacombe House. The path follows the wooded shoreline of the tidal basin known as Millbrook Lake, then climbs steeply inland to reach Maker Church on the highest point of the peninsula. From here you wander through tiny fields to reach a track that leads in a long sweeping descent to the village of Kingsand.

Smugglers' Haven

Kingsand is a charming village, linked seamlessly by the long and narrow Garrett Street to the equally charming Cawsand. These were very successful smugglers' havens during the 18th and early 19th centuries. In Garrett Street, opposite the Halfway House Inn, look for a sign on the wall indicating the old Cornwall-Devon border. The Cornish side of Plymouth Sound was incorporated into Anglo-Saxon territory in 705 AD in order to secure both banks of the estuary against, mainly Viking, raids. Kingsand remained as part of Devon until 1844. From Kingsand the route follows the coastal footpath along the more bracing sea shore of Plymouth Sound. Finally you reach the delightful park environment that surrounds Mount Edgcumbe House where you can visit the house if you wish and explore the lovely gardens.

Walk 7 Directions

① Go left along the footway opposite the car park entrance. Where the footway ends at an old fountain and horse trough, cross back left and go through a gap by a telephone kiosk, signposted 'Empacombe'. Keep left past the Old School Rooms. Turn right at a junction then pass an obelisk and follow the path alongside the tree-hidden creek to Empacombe.

② At a surfaced lane, by a house, keep ahead and go down to Empacombe Quay. Turn left beyond the low wall, (dogs under control please) and skirt the edge of the small harbour to reach a stone stile onto a wooded path. Continue round Palmer Point and on to a public road.

③ Go through the kissing gate opposite, signposted 'Maker Church, Kingsand'. Follow the track ahead for 55yds (50m), then bear right, up the open field (no obvious path) heading between telegraph poles, to find a faint path into Pigshill Wood. Bear right along a track, go left at signposts and climb uphill following footpath signs. Cross a track, then go up some stone steps to reach more steps onto a public road. Cross, with care, and follow a path to Maker Church.

> **WHERE TO EAT AND DRINK** ⓘ
> Kingsand has a number of good pubs, restaurants and cafés. The **Rising Sun** is a pleasant, old style pub. It offers pasties, crab platter and local scallops. The **Halfway House** has some fine beers and does excellent meals with seafood a speciality. On the seafront is **Cleave Tea Rooms**, a licensed restaurant serving fresh crab. In Cremyll the **Edgcumbe Arms** is a traditional quayside inn with a pleasant terrace overlooking Plymouth Sound and offering a good selection of real ales and a varied menu. The **Orangery Restaurant and Tea Room** is located in the Old Orangery in Mount Edgcumbe estate's Italian garden.

④ Turn sharp right in front of the church, follow the field edge, then go over a stile on the left. Follow the next field edge and cross a stile on the left, then follow the path past a house and across a lane into a field. Cross two fields to a lane. Turn up right, then go left at a junction.

⑤ Where the road levels off, bear off left down a track at a public footpath signpost. Keep ahead at a junction and, after a long level stretch, go left at a junction to reach Kingsand via **Devonport Hill** and **Kingsway**. To explore **Kingsand** and **Cawsand**, bear left down the narrow **Heavitree Road**.

⑥ To return to **Cremyll**, at Kingsway go through a gate into **Mount Edgcumbe Country Park**. Follow a good track to a public lane at **Hooe Lake Valley**.

⑦ Rejoin the coast path, signposted just a few paces along the lane. Keep to the upper path at a junction, then merge with another track from the left and continue through the woods.

⑧ A few paces after passing beneath an arch, bear off right from the main track and down a path zig-zagging steeply downhill to the coast. Follow the coast path back to Mount Edgcumbe and **Cremyll**.

> **WHILE YOU'RE THERE** ⓘ
> Mount Edgcumbe House was built in the mid-16th century and subsequently enlarged. It was badly damaged by German incendiary bombs in 1941 and rebuilt in the 1960s. In 1971 house and estate were purchased jointly by Cornwall County Council and Plymouth City Council and the Mount Edgcumbe Country Park was established. The house is open to the public and has a fine collection of mainly modern furnishings and Victorian artefacts. There are paintings by artists such as Sir Joshua Reynolds. The surrounding gardens include the Earl's Garden, an 18th-century formal garden. The house is open, Wed–Sun and Bank Holiday Monday, from April to mid-October.

Rocky Bounds of Bodmin

A moorland walk across the exhilarating wilds of Bodmin Moor.

•DISTANCE•	3 miles (4.8km)
•MINIMUM TIME•	2hrs 30min
•ASCENT / GRADIENT•	230ft (70m) ▲▲ ▲ ▲
•LEVEL OF DIFFICULTY•	🥾🥾 🥾 🥾
•PATHS•	Moorland tracks and paths and disused quarry tramways
•LANDSCAPE•	Open moorland punctuated with rocky tors
•SUGGESTED MAP•	aqua3 OS Explorer 109 Bodmin Moor
•START / FINISH•	Grid reference: SX 260711
•DOG FRIENDLINESS•	Keep under strict control around livestock
•PARKING•	The Hurlers car park on south west side of Minions village
•PUBLIC TOILETS•	Minions village

BACKGROUND TO THE WALK

Walk across London's Westminster Bridge and you walk across Bodmin Moor. Granite used in the fabric of the bridge comes from the now disused granite quarry of the Cheesewring that dominates the eastern section of the moor near the village of Minions. Bodmin Moor granite was also used in London's Albert Memorial and in countless other structures world-wide, including a lighthouse in Sri Lanka. Nineteenth century stone workers extracted granite, not only from the great raw gash of Cheesewring Quarry, but also from the wildest parts of the moor such as the lower slopes of Kilmar Tor, on Twelve Men's Moor, where this walk leads.

Cider Press

Cheesewring Quarry is the torn-open heart of Stowe's Hill. It takes its name from a remarkable granite 'tor', a pile of naturally formed rock that stands on the quarry's lip. The name 'Cheesewring' comes from the tor's fanciful resemblance to a traditional cider press, used to crush apples into a 'cheese'. There are many similar 'cheesewrings' throughout Bodmin Moor, but none so splendid as this one. Such formations were partly formed below ground millions of years ago, and were then exposed when erosion sculpted the landscape. On the way up to the Cheesewring, visit Daniel Gumb's Cave, a reconstructed version of a rock 'house' once occupied by an 18th-century stone worker who was also a self-taught philosopher and mathematician. On the roof you will see a roughly carved theorem, though its authenticity is not proven. Beyond the Cheesewring, the summit of Stowe's Hill is enclosed by an old 'pound', the defining walls of a possible Bronze Age settlement.

Relics of a much older society than that of the quarry workers' are found at the very start of the walk, where you pass the stone circles called The Hurlers. These are remnants of Bronze Age ceremonial sites, though a later culture created fanciful tales of the pillars, and those of the nearby 'Pipers'. It's said they were men turned to stone for playing the Cornish ball-throwing sport of hurling on a Sunday – to the sound of music. Relish the names, but reflect on the more intriguing Bronze Age realities. Beyond the Cheesewring and The Hurlers, the walk will take you through a compelling landscape, along the granite 'setts' or slabs of disused quarry tramways, and past lonely tors at the heart of Bodmin Moor.

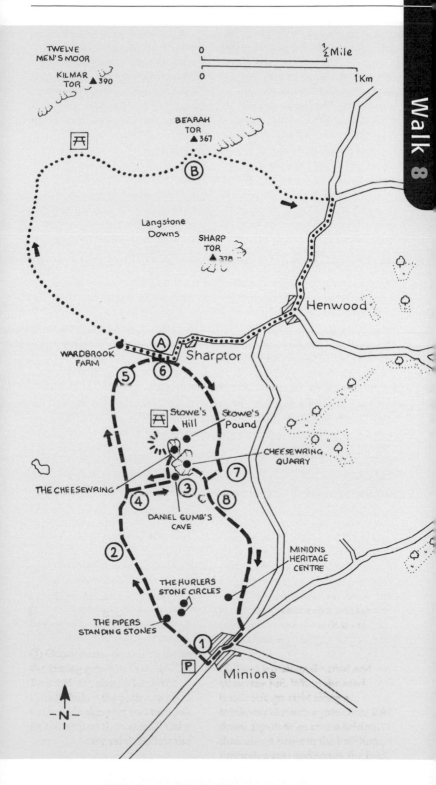

Walk 8 Directions

① Leave the car park by steps at its top end beside an information board about **The Hurlers stone circles**. Cross the grass to a broad stony track. Turn right and follow the track, passing The Hurlers circles on the right and the **Pipers stones** further on.

② At a three-way junction, by a large granite block, take the right-hand track down through a shallow valley bottom, then climb uphill on a green track towards **Cheesewring Quarry**. At a junction with another track, cross over and follow a grassy track uphill towards the quarry. At the first green hillock, go sharp right, then round left to find **Daniel Gumb's Cave** (➤ Background to the Walk). Return to the path and follow it uphill alongside the fenced-in rim of the quarry to the Cheesewring rock formation.

WHAT TO LOOK FOR   ⓘ

The stone setts of the old tramways are the most obvious reminders of Bodmin's stone-cutting industry, but you'll also see the remains of buildings and granite ramps from which stone was loaded into wagons. The boulders and little 'cheesewrings' of Stowe's Hill and Kilmar Tor were protected from quarrying and on Stowe's Hill especially, near the edge of Cheesewring Quarry, you may be lucky to spot the elegant motif of a fleur-de-lis carved into boulders, a mark used to designate the limits of quarrying and stone cutting.

---

③ Retrace your steps towards the shallow valley bottom.

④ A short distance from the valley bottom, abreast of some thorn trees on the right and just before a fenced-off mound on the left, turn off right along a path. Keep left of the thorn trees and a big leaning block of granite and soon pick up the faint beginnings of a grassy track. Follow this track, keeping to the right of a solitary thorn tree and some gorse bushes. The track soon becomes much clearer.

⑤ The track begins to strand. At a leaning rock, split like a whale's mouth, keep right along a path through scrub and with the rocky heights of **Sharp Tor** in line ahead. Keep to the path round the slope, with **Wardbrook Farm** left and **Sharp Tor** ahead. Reach a surfaced road and turn right for a few paces to reach an open gateway.

⑥ Go to the right of the fence by the gateway and follow a path alongside the fence past two slim granite pillars. Join a disused tramway and follow this.

⑦ Pass some big piles of broken rock and, about 30yds (27m) beyond them, turn sharp right at a wall corner. Follow a green track uphill and alongside a wall. Where the wall ends keep on uphill to reach a broad track.

⑧ Turn right along the track if you want to visit Cheesewring Quarry. For the main route, turn left and follow the track to **Minions village**. Pass the **Minions Heritage Centre**, a converted mine engine house. At the main road, turn right through the village to return to the **car park**.

WHILE YOU'RE THERE   ⓘ

Bodmin Moor was exploited below ground as well as above. Its story is told at the **Minions Heritage Centre** in the refurbished Houseman's Engine House, once used to pump water from the South Pheonix Mine.

More Tors and Lonely Moorland

An extension to Walk 8 delves further into Bodmin's granite upland.
See map and information panel for Walk 8

•DISTANCE•	6½ miles (10.4km)
•MINIMUM TIME•	4hrs
•ASCENT / GRADIENT•	558ft (170m) 🔺🔺🔺
•LEVEL OF DIFFICULTY•	🚶🚶 🚶🚶 🚶

Walk 9 Directions (Walk 8 option)

On Walk 8 at Point ⑥, go left along the surfaced road. About 80yds (73m) before **Wardbrook Farm** go off right by a line of tumbled boulders and then turn left along the raised surface of a disused tramway. You now need to go through several gates in order to pass to the right of Wardbrook Farm, Point Ⓐ. Please be absolutely certain that if you need to open any of these gates you close them securely behind you. Soon you should reach the open moor along the stony track of the tramway that served the various granite cutting areas scattered across the lonely reaches of **Twelve Men's Moor**. The tramway passes below the great dragon-backed ridge of **Kilmar Tor**, a glorious half-mile (800m) of huge, wind-sculpted boulders and piled blocks. Where the tramway forks, keep right, and continue to **Bearah Tor Quarry**.

In sight of Bearah Tor Quarry you need to be careful with your route finding through the scrub. Where the track forks by some raised

granite blocks, Point Ⓑ, keep to the lower fork and head towards the piled rocks of the quarry. A few feet in front of the rocks, step down right and follow a grassy track round the edge of the rocks to cross some very wet, reedy ground – it is much drier close to an old concrete shelter – to reach a track. Turn right and follow the track to where it reaches a surfaced lane. Turn right and follow the lane to the pretty hamlet of **Henwood**.

Keep downhill into Henwood and, at a junction by a telephone box, turn right, signposted '**Sharptor and Minions**' and begin a steady uphill climb. Keep right at the next junction. Brace yourself for a really steep climb until the lane levels off above **Sharptor** hamlet where you reach the gateway at Point ⑥ once more, from where you follow directions on Walk 8.

ⓘ WHERE TO EAT AND DRINK

There are no refreshment points anywhere on the moor, nor at the hamlets of Henwood or Sharptor. You are advised to take food and drink with you. The **Cheesewring Hotel and Pub** at Minions does meals and the **Hurlers Halt** and Minions Tearooms do coffee, tea and meals.

The Looe River Valleys by Rail and Ramble

A short journey by rail leads to a leisurely walk along country lanes and riverside paths.

·DISTANCE·	6½ miles (10.4km)
·MINIMUM TIME·	3hrs 20min
·ASCENT / GRADIENT·	197ft (60m) ▲▲▲
·LEVEL OF DIFFICULTY·	🚶 🚶 🚶
·PATHS·	Good woodland, riverside paths, tracks and quiet lanes. Can be very muddy on riverside sections
·LANDSCAPE·	Fields, riverbank and woodland
·SUGGESTED MAP·	aqua3 OS Map Explorer 107 St Austell & Liskeard
·START·	Grid reference: SX 249591
·FINISH·	Millpool Car Park, West Looe. Grid reference: SX 250538
·DOG FRIENDLINESS·	Notices indicate where dogs must be on lead
·PARKING·	Millpool Car Park, West Looe, across river bridge from East Looe. Looe Station ½ mile (800m) from Millpool car park, reached by crossing river bridge then walking north along A387 (Small car park at Looe Station is much dearer)
·PUBLIC TOILETS·	Duloe
·NOTE·	The Looe Valley Line, Liskeard–Looe. Request halts at Coombe, St Keyne, Causeland, and Sandplace. Tell the conductor your destination for request stop halts. 8–9 trains both ways, each day

Walk 10 Directions

This walk begins with a short, stress-free train ride from busy **Looe** to the serenity of **Causeland Station Halt** in the valley of the East Looe River. Once the train has gone, enjoy the tranquillity of this tiny 'one-horse' stop. With its electronic information point it may not be entirely Betjamenesque, but it is close. On leaving the station, turn immediately left along a quiet lane to a junction with another lane opposite **Badham Farm Holiday Cottages**. Brace yourself for a stiff climb for the next ¼ mile (400m). The effort is worth it; you gain

height and then the rest of the route is generally downhill all the way. In ¾ mile (1.2km) go left over a stone stile, turn right through a gap and then head diagonally across a field towards the opposite right-hand corner and a row of houses. (If the field is under crops and no right-of-way apparent, you may have to go round the field edge). Go through a

---

> **WHERE TO EAT AND DRINK** ⓘ
> **Ye Olde Plough House Inn** at Duloe is a classic village inn with oak beams, open fires and flagstone floors and with a pleasant garden area. Imaginative food includes leek and mushroom crumble, and baguettes with tasty fillings. Sharps' Doom Bar is a fine ale.

WHAT TO LOOK FOR

In the more open valley below Sowden's Bridge, **buzzards** can often be seen wheeling through the sky. The buzzard is more scavenger than raptor; its prey includes small birds, lizards, snakes, frogs and even earth worms and it will happily eat insects and other birds' eggs. Crows and gulls will often mob a buzzard relentlessly. The buzzard's response is usually a lazy indifference, but if pushed too far, it will flip over onto its back with its ferocious talons unsheathed.

gap in the far hedge, just left of the field corner, then turn right and go through a field gate and down a lane to the main road. There are public toilets along to the right. Opposite is the post office and village shop. Go left along the footway to reach the welcoming **Olde Plough House Inn**, preferably in time for lunch.

Continue along the main road from the pub and in about 275yds (251m) you'll reach a signpost indicating the way to the **Duloe Stone Circle**. This haunting Bronze Age ceremonial site is composed of eight quartzite stones, each one representing the main points of the compass. Take the opportunity of checking your directional instincts – and your compass. Once back on the main road, walk the few paces to Duloe's **Church of St Cuby**.

Leave the churchyard by the top gateway into the lane alongside the village war memorial. Turn right and follow the lane, past the village green and school, for ¼ mile (1.2km). Keep ahead past a junction on the right and descend steeply into the wooded valley of the **West Looe River**. Go left at a T-junction. As the trees close gently round you here and, just before reaching the

river, go left over a stile by a gate. Do not follow the track directly ahead; instead bear right at a signpost and follow a grassy path that becomes a broad track above the river. Follow the well-signposted riverside way for the next ¾ mile (1.2km) in tandem with the chuckling river to reach a narrow lane at **Sowden's Bridge**.

Turn right here, then cross the bridge and follow the lane, ignoring side junctions but going left at a final three-way junction, signed '**Kilminorth and Watergate**'. In ½ mile (800m), turn left by some pretty cottages into the nature reserve of **Kilminorth Woods**. These ancient oak woods were once 'coppiced', the trees being cut back to a stump and the resulting clusters of new shoots harvested for hedging and other uses. You can choose your route through the woods to **Looe**, either by following a lower riverside footpath, or the higher **Giant's Hedge** footpath that first climbs steeply uphill, then follows the line of the vegetated Giant's Hedge, probably a 6th-century boundary dyke that marked out the territory of a local chieftain. Both routes are well-signposted and take you pleasantly back to **Millpool car park**.

WHILE YOU'RE THERE

Visit Duloe's **Church of St Cuby** whose tower leans noticeably. The lean was so acute that the top storey was removed in the 1860s. One reason given for the lean was that the huge amount of smuggled goods hidden in the tower had caused the supporting walls to sag. The story of the ancient water basin inside the church is told on an accompanying notice. The gravestones near the access gate are a graphic and brutal record of the child mortality of the 19th century.

Walk 11

Between Moors and Meadows at Camelford

Riverside, woodland and quiet fields in sight of wild moorland make up this charming circuit in North Cornwall.

•DISTANCE•	5 miles (8km)
•MINIMUM TIME•	3hrs
•ASCENT / GRADIENT•	164ft (50m) ▲▲ ▲▲ ▲▲
•LEVEL OF DIFFICULTY•	충충 충충 충충
•PATHS•	Obvious, well-marked paths. Some field sections poorly defined, 28 stiles, some in triplicate and very high
•LANDSCAPE•	Wooded riverside, fields and quiet lanes
•SUGGESTED MAP•	aqua3 OS Explorer 109 Bodmin Moor
•START / FINISH•	Grid reference: SX 106836
•DOG FRIENDLINESS•	Dogs on lead through grazed areas. May find high, multiple stiles difficult
•PARKING•	Church car park at north entrance to Camelford, or small car park opposite the North Cornwall Museum
•PUBLIC TOILETS•	Entrance to Enfield Park, Camelford, near Church car park. Car park opposite North Cornwall Museum

BACKGROUND TO THE WALK

Camelford qualifies as a moorland 'capital', yet its immediate surroundings are entirely unmoorlike in character. The town nestles in a river valley on the western side of Bodmin Moor and the unexpected views of bare and rocky moorland hills seen during this walk are a pleasing contrast to the lush green countryside that surrounds the town. Camelford has a long and distinguished history. It originated as a strategic river crossing and was granted a Royal Charter as early as the 13th century, giving it the right to hold markets and fairs. The old coaching road to the west skirted the raw uplands of Bodmin Moor and passed through Camelford. Today the town retains its strong historical character although it is partly robbed of inherent charm by incessant through-traffic. A main road still squeezes through what is still, in terms of its narrow streets, the medieval heart of Camelford. Remarkably, however, the start of this walk delivers you instantly into leafy riverside shade and peace and quiet.

Riverside Paths

From Camelford's Town Hall you cross the narrow Fore Street and pass through an arched passageway called 'The Moors', another indication of an older Camelford that had immediate references to the great sweep of Bodmin Moor to the east. But here it is all wooded riverside paths that take you downstream alongside the River Camel. After half a mile (800m) or so, the route climbs away from the river through quiet meadows, including a wonderful trout pond meadow at Trethin, to reach the handsome Advent Church of St Athwenna. This is a fine isolated position for a church, but sadly St Athwenna's suffers because of this risky isolation and is kept locked, to guard against theft and vandalism.

Rocky Ridge

From the church the route leads through fields and along quiet lanes with unexpected views of the dragon-backed rocky ridge of Roughtor (pronounced Rowtor) and its higher neighbouring hill the more rounded Brown Willy, the highest point in Cornwall at 1,377ft (419 metres). At Watergate, you pass through an intriguing area of old walls and terraces that may have been part of a mill complex; today the walls are muffled with velvety moss, the ground is thick with lush grass. Soon higher ground is reached at Moorgate, another name echoing the area's domination by Bodmin Moor. From here you head back towards Camelford, passing along some engagingly muddy lanes on the way.

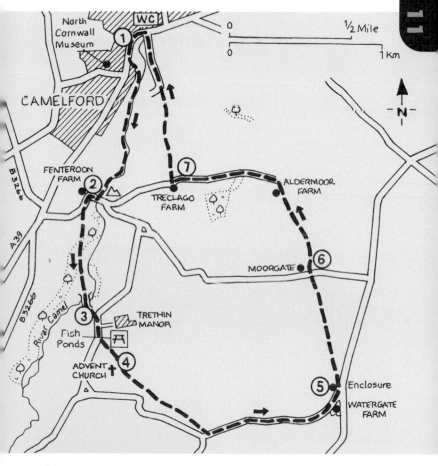

Walk 11 Directions

① From between the **Town Hall** and the **Darlington Inn**, cross the main street, with care, and turn up **Fore Street** for a few paces. Go left through a low archway, signed 'The Moors', and signposted 'To The River and Advent Church'. Follow the riverside path downstream.

② At a surfaced lane and beside a bridge, turn right and uphill. At the top of a steep incline, just before **Fenteroon Farm**, go left and through a gate, signposted '**Public Footpath**'. Follow the first field edge then cross the next field. Go over a very high stile and descend through woods towards the river. Ignore the stile first passed on the right and instead keep down to a signpost in the valley bottom. Cross the meadow ahead, then go left over a bridge and through a tangle of trees. Bear steeply up left, then go left again, by a signpost, to reach a stile into a lane.

③ Turn right, then, just past the entrance to **Trethin Manor**, bear off left over a stile, and go through a pleasant meadow and past a fish pond. Cross a granite clapper bridge and a stile, then go up the field to **Advent churchyard**.

WHAT TO LOOK FOR ℹ️

Keep your eyes peeled as soon as you start walking down the riverside path and you may spot the intriguing dipper, a small dark brown, almost black bird with an unmistakable white patch on its breast. The dipper haunts streams and can stay under water for a time, braced against the stream's flow while seeking out aquatic insects, water snails, larvae and even tiny fish. It can also 'swim' under water, using its wings.

---

④ From the east end of the churchyard, (on the opposite side of church to where you entered the churchyard) go over a wooden stile and slightly right across a field, to several stiles. Cross a meadow then follow right-hand field edges to three stiles in the hedge. Bear left across the middle of the next field to its far corner and into a surfaced lane. Turn left along the lane.

⑤ Turn left just before the stream and T-junction by **Watergate Farm**. Go over stiles and alongside the stream on stone flags. Pass a little enclosure, follow the stream for a

---

WHERE TO EAT AND DRINK ℹ️

There are no refreshment opportunities on the route of the walk, but Camelford has many food outlets. There are a number of cafés and restaurants. The **Mason's Arms** and the **Darlington Inn** both do bar meals.

---

short distance, then skirt high gorse and fenced-in trees to reach hidden stiles into a field. Go straight up the field slope and continue to a stile into the next field. Continue to the lane at **Moorgate**.

⑥ Cross the lane, go through several fields and then continue along a stony track to reach another lane at **Aldermoor Farm**. Turn left along the lane.

⑦ Turn right opposite buildings at Treclago Farm, and go up a lane. At a junction, keep straight ahead along a track. This section can be extremely muddy and mucky. Descend a meadow to a gate, cross a wooden footbridge over a stream, then climb steeply uphill to reach a surfaced lane. Follow the lane, **College Road**, to reach **Camelford**.

WHILE YOU'RE THERE ℹ️

Enjoy a visit to the excellent **North Cornwall Museum** in Clease Road, Camelford, the road that leads off right from the top end of Fore Street. Then walk down the adjacent Chapel Street with its cobbled rainwater gullies and look at the town's historic buildings such as the **Town Hall**, which has a weather vane in the form of a golden camel. The nearby **Darlington Inn** has 16th-century features, and although the interior was destroyed by fire in 1995, much has been restored to its original state. At the north end of Market Place is the attractive **Enfield Park**.

Through the Woods to Cardinham Church

A long woodland walk in quiet countryside between Bodmin town and Bodmin Moor.

•DISTANCE•	5 miles (8km)
•MINIMUM TIME•	3hrs 30min
•ASCENT / GRADIENT•	328ft (100m) ▲ ▲ ▲
•LEVEL OF DIFFICULTY•	👥 👥 👥
•PATHS•	Generally clear woodland tracks and field sections, 6 stiles
•LANDSCAPE•	Deep woodland of deciduous and conifer trees, quiet meadows
•SUGGESTED MAP•	aqua3 OS Explorer 109 Bodmin Moor
•START / FINISH•	Grid reference: SX 099666
•DOG FRIENDLINESS•	Dogs on lead through grazed areas. The woodland management requests that dogs don't foul the picnic areas
•PARKING•	Cardinham Woods car park
•PUBLIC TOILETS•	At car park

BACKGROUND TO THE WALK

Cardinham Woods occupy a favoured position, east of Bodmin town, in the serene countryside drained by the Cardinham Water and its tributaries. The 650 acres (263ha) that make up the combined Deviock, Hurtstocks, Callywith and Tawnamoor Woods of Cardinham have been in the hands of the Forestry Commission since 1922. The original woodland was used for a number of traditional rural industries including charcoal burning. Some of the old woodland of oak, beech, hazel, birch, and holly, survives. The commercial timber includes larch, Sitka spruce and Douglas fir. Most of the tracks and paths throughout the woods are courtesy of the woodland management and visitors must always heed notices indicating where work is being carried out.

Peaceful Hamlet

There are a number of waymarked, themed trails throughout the Cardinham Forestry area, but this walk takes you beyond the woods to the peaceful hamlet of Cardinham and to its handsome church of St Meubred's. From the well-appointed parking and picnic area at the entrance to Cardinham Woods the way leads along a broad forestry track above the Cardinham Water to a major junction of tracks at Ladyvale Bridge. You turn immediately left before the bridge, but before doing so, walk on for a few paces past a big signpost and look at the little granite 'clapper' bridge that crosses the rushing stream down on the right. Now blocked off this was known as Valebridge and was a major crossing point for centuries. Somewhere within the tangle of woodland behind the bridge is the site of Ladyvale Chapel, an early Christian site. The bridge is a rather poignant reminder of a less mannered world than our own.

As you climb higher into the woods, the route leaves the managed forest and passes through the upper reaches of Lidcutt Wood, a glorious witch-world of old beech trees whose

Walk 12

moss-covered trunks are entwined with thick columns of menacing ivy that will send a shiver up your spine, if not your legs. Beyond here a quiet lane descends steeply to a field path that leads up to the Church of St Meubred (► While You're There). From the church you head back towards Cardinham Woods through old meadows and along ancient tracks that once served as a pilgrims' way to Ladyvale Chapel.

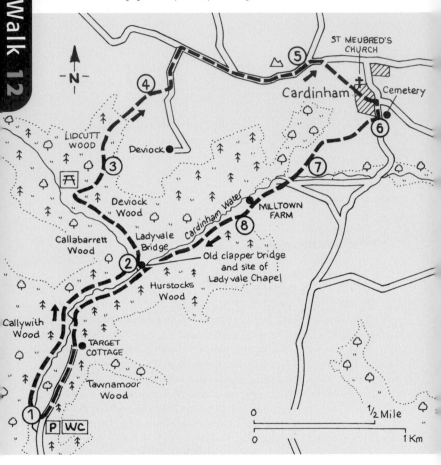

Walk 12 Directions

① From the **Cardinham Woods car park**, head for the the west side of the main bridge over the **Cardinham Water** and bear right through a wooden barrier to a three-way junction. Keep to the right and follow a broad forestry track through the woods with the Cardinham Water down to your right.

② At a junction of tracks, keep right and cross a hidden tributary stream that descends from the left, then turn immediately left up a track. Soon, pass picnic tables by a little rock face on a bend.

③ Turn off right at a junction and pass a purple marker post. In a few paces, at the next junction, keep straight ahead along a grassy track through **Lidcutt Wood**. Go over a stile and on through woods.

④ Emerge into a field and turn sharply right and uphill by a signpost to reach a gate onto a concrete track. Turn left and follow the track to a public road. Turn right along the road and follow it over the brow of the hill and down into the valley.

WHERE TO EAT AND DRINK ⓘ

There are no food and drink outlets on the route. There was a delightful riverside café at the Cardinham Woods reception area, but it is closed and there is no certainty, at present, that it will reopen as a café. You will find a range of food outlets in Bodmin 4 miles (6.5km) away, but if you want an authentic country pub try the London Inn at St Neot, 8 miles to the east of Cardinham Woods.

---

⑤ A few paces beyond a junction, pass a public footpath sign, cross a river then go off right at another public footpath sign. Cross a little ditch and go over a stile. Head diagonally up the field, aiming to the right of **Cardinham church tower**, to reach a stile. Go along a grassy ride beside the church. Turn right at the road.

WHILE YOU'RE THERE ⓘ

St Meubred's Church at Cardinham village is a handsome building both inside and out. The churchyard boasts two splendid Cornish crosses one of which is well over 8ft (2m) high. The aisles have very fine wagon roofs, some of which retain original colouring, and are more than matched by the 15th–16th century bench ends. During the Second World War, St Meubred's was damaged by a bomb, meant for Plymouth. It landed in the churchyard and destroyed the chancel windows.

---

⑥ At a public footpath sign opposite a cemetery, go right and through a gate into a field. Keep parallel to a fence, then turn left in front of a house and follow an overgrown old track, keeping to the left of a tree. Go through a wooden gate and keep alongside the hedge on the right. Where the track bends round right, bear off left and downhill between trees, and cross a meadow to a stile. This is the line of the right of way. There may be notices here inviting you to keep to the right-hand edge of the field all the way round to the stile.

WHAT TO LOOK FOR ⓘ

If you are very lucky – and very quiet – you may spot the elusive roe deer. This is a small, handsome little deer with red-brown summer coat and long grey winter coat. The small antlers are very upright and usually have only three points.

---

⑦ Bear slightly to the left across the next field to a wooden gate beside a horse jump. Keep ahead through a meadow to a bridge over a stream by a water jump, then follow a path through the trees. Go through a wooden gate and reach a T-junction with a track at **Milltown**. Turn right here, down a surfaced lane and keep left at a junction. Pass **Milltown Farm**, then pass a junction on the left and reach a black and white wooden barrier. Go up a slope, then turn right at a junction with a forestry track.

⑧ Follow the track, and then a surfaced lane from **Target Cottage**, to the car park.

Walk 13

A Glimpse of Old Cornwall at Polruan

A woodland and coastal walk from the village of Polruan through the ancient parish of Lanteglos.

•DISTANCE•	4 miles (6.4km)
•MINIMUM TIME•	3hrs 30min
•ASCENT / GRADIENT•	754ft (230m) ▲▲▲
•LEVEL OF DIFFICULTY•	🚶🚶 🚶🚶 🚶🚶
•PATHS•	Good throughout. Can be very muddy in woodland areas during wet weather
•LANDSCAPE•	Deep woodland alongside tidal creek. Open coastal cliffs
•SUGGESTED MAP•	aqua3 OS Explorer 107 St Austell & Liskeard
•START / FINISH•	Grid reference: SX 126511
•DOG FRIENDLINESS•	Dogs on lead through grazed areas. Notices indicate
•PARKING•	Polruan. An alternative start to the walk can be made from the National Trust Pencarrow car park (► ④, SX 149513) . You can also park at Fowey's Central car park, then catch the ferry to Polruan
•PUBLIC TOILETS•	Polruan

BACKGROUND TO THE WALK

There are parts of Cornwall so encompassed by the sea that they seem genuinely out of this modern world. The sea, rather than the dual carriageway, is still their major highway. The village of Polruan on the estuary of the River Fowey is one such place. The green headland on which it stands has the sea on its southern shore and is bounded to the north by the wonderfully calm and tree-lined tidal creek of Pont Pill. The village can be reached by land only along fairly minor roads that detour at some length from Cornwall's main spinal highways. Yet Polruan lies only a few hundred yards (metres) across the estuary from the bustling town of Fowey and a regular passenger ferry runs between the two.

Old Cornwall

Polruan and its surrounding parish of Lanteglos are redolent of old Cornwall. Prehistoric settlers found a natural refuge on the narrow headland on which it stands. Christian 'saints' and medieval worshippers set up chantries and chapels in the sheltered hollows; merchants prospered from the lucrative sea trade into Fowey's natural harbour. During the wars of the 14th and 15th centuries, Fowey ships harried foreign vessels, and because of their outstanding seamanship, earned themselves the admiring sobriquet of 'Fowey Gallants'. The entrance to the estuary was protected from attack by a chain barrier that could be winched across the river's mouth from blockhouses on either bank. In peacetime the Gallants continued to raid shipping of all types until Edward IV responded to complaints from foreign merchants, and several English ones, by confiscating ships and by having the protective chain removed. Resilient as always, the seaman of Fowey and Polruan turned their hands successfully to fishing and smuggling instead.

Walk 13

The route of this walk starts from Polruan. It wanders through peaceful countryside that was once owned by wealthy medieval families who played a major part in organising the freebooting activities of Polruan seamen. Original fortunes made through piracy were turned to legitimate trade and to farming and land management and the delightful countryside through which the walk leads is the product of long term land ownership and rural trade. At its heart lies the splendid Lanteglos Church of St Winwaloe, or St Willow. The second part of the walk leads back to the sea, to the steep headland of Pencarrow and to the dramatic amphitheatre of Lantic Bay with its splendid beach, an old smugglers domain if ever there was one. From here, the coastal footpath leads airily back to Polruan and to the rattle and hum of an estuary that has never ceased to be alive with seagoing.

Walk 13 Directions

① Walk up from **the Quay** at Polruan, then turn left along **East Street**, by a telephone box and a seat. Go right, up steps, signposted '**To the Hills**' and '**Hall Walk**'.

Go left at the next junction, then keep along the path ahead. Keep right at a junction and pass a National Trust sign, '**North Downs**'.

② Turn right at a T-junction with a track, then in just a few paces, bear off left along a path, signposted

'**Pont and Bodinnick**'. Reach a wooden gate onto a lane. Don't go through the gate, but instead bear left and go over a stile. Follow a path, established by the National Trust, and eventually descend steep wooden steps.

WHAT TO LOOK FOR ⓘ

Spend some time exploring **Polruan**, at the beginning or end of the walk. This fine little port has retained much of its vernacular character in spite of some modern development. Polruan thrived because of seagoing and there is still a rich sense of those sea-dominated days in the narrow alleyways of the village.

---

③ At a T-junction with a track, turn right and climb uphill. It's worth diverting left at the T-junction to visit **Pont** (► Walk 14). On this route reach a lane. Go left for a few paces then, on a bend by **Little Churchtown Farm**, bear off right through a gate signed '**Footpath to Church**'. Climb steadily to reach the **Church of St Winwaloe**.

④ Turn left outside the church and follow a narrow lane. At a T-junction, just beyond **Pencarrow car park**, cross the road

---

WHILE YOU'RE THERE ⓘ

The handsome **Church of St Winwaloe**, or Willow, has notable wagon roofs containing some original 14th-century timbers as well as many other beams added during later centuries. The side walls and piers lean engagingly to either side. The novelist Daphne du Maurier was married here in 1932 and the church features as 'Lanoc Church' in her book *The Loving Spirit*.

---

and go through a gate, then turn right along the field edge on a path established by the National Trust, to go through another gate. Turn left along the field edge.

⑤ At the field corner, turn right onto the coast path and descend very steeply. (To continue to **Pencarrow Head** go left over the stile here and follow the path onto the headland. From here the coast path can be re-joined and access made to **Great Lantic Beach**.) Follow the coast path for about 1¼ miles (2km), keeping to the cliff edge ignoring any junctions.

WHERE TO EAT AND DRINK ⓘ

There are no refreshment opportunities on the walk, but the **Russell Inn** at the bottom of Fore Street, Polruan and the **Lugger Inn** on Polruan Quay, both do good pub lunches. There are a number of cafés and restaurants in Polruan. The **Old Ferry Inn** at Bodinnick also does pub lunches.

---

⑥ Where the cliff path ends, go through a gate to a road junction. Cross the road then go down **School Lane**. Turn right at '**Speakers Corner**', then turn left down Fore Street to reach **the Quay** at Polruan.

Across Pont Pill to Penleath Point

Continue around the inlet of Pont Pill to Pont and the ancient Hall Chapel.
See map and information panel for Walk 13

•DISTANCE•	2 miles (3.2km) for this loop
•MINIMUM TIME•	1hr 30min
•ASCENT / GRADIENT•	311ft (95m) ▲▲ ▲▲ ▲
•LEVEL OF DIFFICULTY•	犳 犳 犳
•START / FINISH•	Grid reference: SX 144519
•PUBLIC TOILETS•	Bodinnick

Walk 14 Directions (Walk 13 option)

An extension can be added to Walk 13 by crossing the head of **Pont Pill**, just down from the junction on the main walk at Point ③. It is hard to resist, once you've diverted to the charming creekside settlement of picturesque Pont. A little footbridge beckons; the wooded heights opposite draw you on; good things are hidden amidst the trees. At Pont are the remains of a lime kiln indicating that the quay here was once busy with sailing barges offloading limestone, sand and coal, and carrying away grain, timber and farm produce, worthier, if more mundane trades, than piracy and smuggling.

Once across the bridge, at Point Ⓐ, bear right along the path, sign-posted **Bodinnick**. Turn left at a T-junction and climb up through the trees of the **Grove** and emerge onto open fields. Go diagonally left across the first field, then go through a gate and follow the next field edge to another gate. Go along the right-hand edge of the next field and through the middle gate of three onto a track. Soon pass the ruins of the 14th-century **Hall Chapel**. On a bend just beyond the chapel, go through a gate into a field. Keep straight ahead and follow the right-hand hedge to a wooden stile. Beyond the stile, at Point Ⓑ, join the **Hall Walk** path, by a war memorial.

Turn right if you want to visit **Bodinnick**, another settlement on the tidal River Fowey that played an important part in the history of the area. On the main route, turn left along **Hall Walk**, a 16th-century estate promenade. Follow Hall Walk round **Penleath Point** to where a granite memorial commemorates the novelist Arthur Quiller Couch who wrote under the pen name of 'Q'. He lived for many years in the area and immortalised the town of Fowey as 'Troy Town' in his novels. Continue through the woods and eventually reach a stile into a field above the Grove. From here you can retrace your earlier route back to **Pont**.

Quarrymen and Kings at Tintagel

A tour of the spectacular coastal quarries between Tintagel and Trebarwith Strand.

•DISTANCE•	3 miles (4.8km)
•MINIMUM TIME•	2hrs
•ASCENT / GRADIENT•	197ft (60m) ▲ ▲▲ ▲
•LEVEL OF DIFFICULTY•	🚶🚶 🚶🚶 🚶🚶
•PATHS•	Good coastal paths and field paths, 13 stiles
•LANDSCAPE•	Spectacular sea cliff quarries
•SUGGESTED MAP•	aqua3 OS Explorer 111 Bude, Boscastle and Tintagel
•START / FINISH•	Grid reference: SX 056885
•DOG FRIENDLINESS•	Dogs on lead through grazed areas
•PARKING•	Several car parks in Tintagel
•PUBLIC TOILETS•	Tintagel, Trebarwith Strand

Walk 15 **Directions**

If you're looking for myth, Merlin and mystification, then Tintagel on the North Cornish coast offers the lot. Tintagel and its ruined castle on the spectacular headland known as **the Island**, is the centre of a resilient King Arthur industry based on Victorian romanticism and a few scraps of historical wishful thinking. In many ways, the real 'kings' of the Tintagel area were the coastal quarryworkers who extracted slate from the area's great cliffs. Their reign lasted from

---

WHAT TO LOOK FOR ⓘ

The whole area above the quarries and inland has stone walls of slate laid in herringbone pattern and known locally as **curzyway**. There is a good example of such a wall above Lanterdan Quarry and Pinnacle. Keep an eye out for the old platforms at the top of the cliffs that once supported wooden gantries used for lowering slates to ships below.

---

medieval times until the early 20th century and this walk along the rim of the cliff quarries celebrates their memory.

You leave the bustle of Tintagel a few paces from the approach lane to the castle, by turning left down a lane alongside the **Cornishman Inn**, signposted 'St Materiana's Church and Glebe Cliff'. Descend steeply into immediate leafy peace, then, where the rising lane turns sharply right, leave the lane and go over a stile. Continue to a gate and stile, then go through the next field, bearing right across a narrow field to a stile. Continue alongside the right-hand edges of small fields, (dogs under strict control here) to reach a stile into a lane. Follow the lane to a junction of tracks at **Trevillick Farm**, then keep straight across, signposted 'Coast Path'.

Pass two houses and keep ahead to where the track ends at a field gate and stile by final houses. Cross

Walk 15

fields ahead to reach a junction
with the coastal footpath. Go left
along the coast path for a short
distance to reach a junction with a
track inland. From behind a secure
wall you can look down at the
Lanterdan Pinnacle, a tower of
uncut rock rising to 80ft (24m) that
was left in place by quarryworkers
because of its inferior slate. (The
route returns north from here, but
you can, if you wish, continue along
the coast path from **Lanterdan
Quarry** for ½ mile (800m) to
descend to **Trebarwith Strand** and
then return to rejoin the main
walk). On the main walk retrace
your steps from above Lanterdan
Quarry to where the path you
previously followed from **Trevillick
Farm** joins the coast path. Here take
the left branch and follow the path
to reach a gap in a wall on **Bagalow
Cliff**. Bear left here, signposted
'**Permitted Coast Path**', go over a
stile then follow the path round
Penhallic Point

On the tip of the Point a secure
timber platform once projected
from the cliff edge; trimmed slates
were lowered from the platform to
cargo ships that lay alongside the
base of the cliffs in calm weather.
The path now leads past a series of

cliffside workings at **Gull Point
Quarry** and **Lambshouse Quarry**.
At these quarries men were lowered
down the sheer cliff face on ropes to
work out good slate from just above
the tideline. Don't dwell for too
long on the realities of such
everyday work as you follow the
path to join a broad track that
leads down to **Tintagel Youth
Hostel**, once the offices of the
nearby cliff quarries.

Go past the hostel then bear up
right along a track to join a wider
track. Keep left along this track with
the **Church of St Materiana** in sight
(▶ While You're There). Turn left
just before the church and follow a
track along the seaward wall of the
churchyard. Remain on this path
towards the great headland of **the
Island** and its famous ruins to reach
a stile and a path that descends past
big pinnacles of rock to reach the
approach to the castle. Go left here,
if you want to visit the castle, or go
down some steps and then turn
right and follow a valleyside path to
reach the road that leads steeply
uphill to **Tintagel**.

Rollercoaster Path to Port Quin

An exhilarating hike between the North Cornish villages of Port Isaac and Port Quin.

•DISTANCE•	6 miles (9.7km)
•MINIMUM TIME•	4hrs
•ASCENT / GRADIENT•	984ft (300m) ▲▲▲
•LEVEL OF DIFFICULTY•	👫 👫 👫
•PATHS•	Good coastal and field paths. Several sections of coast path run very close to unguarded cliff edges. May not be suitable for children and dogs. 14 stiles
•LANDSCAPE•	Coastal scenery and inland fields, one wooded valley
•SUGGESTED MAP•	aqua3 OS Explorer 106 Newquay and Padstow
•START / FINISH•	Grid reference: SW 999809
•DOG FRIENDLINESS•	On leads in grazed areas
•PARKING•	Port Isaac. Large car park on outskirts of village, can be busy in summer. Allowed on Port Isaac's stony beach, but this is tidal and you need to know tides or you may end up with an amphibious auto. Small car park at Port Quin
•PUBLIC TOILETS•	Port Isaac car park and at start of Roscarrock Hill

BACKGROUND TO THE WALK

The North Cornish coast between the sea inlets of Port Isaac and Port Quin is a marvellous chaos of tumbled cliffs and convoluted hills. The price of all this, for the keen walker, is a strenuous passage along the coastal footpath between the two. You rise and fall like a dipping gull, but without the same ease and effortlessness. The inland return, across fields, to Port Isaac, is undramatic but is not strenuous. On the coastal section, be prepared for airy clifftop paths that in places are pinned narrowly between thin air on the unprotected seaward edge and a lengthy stretch of wooden fencing inland, said by ironic locals to be as visible from space as the Great Wall of China.

Port Isaac

The North Cornish village of Port Isaac is one of the West Country's most popular visitor destinations. The appeal of Port Isaac, however, lies partly in its relative freedom from too many visitors' vehicles. The village is enclosed between the steep slopes of a narrow valley that reaches the sea at a protected inlet, a natural haven for vessels. It is this orientation to the sea that has produced the densely compact nature of the village. The sea was the common highway here, long before the modern road became so; until the early 20th century trading ships brought coal, limestone, timber and other commodities to Port Isaac and carried away, fish, farm produce, mineral ore and building stone.

It's worth taking a little time to explore the village of Port Isaac (➤ While You're There) before setting off uphill on the coastal footpath. The path leads round the smooth-browed Lobber Point, then traces a remarkable rollercoaster route along the folded coastline to

Kellan Head and then to Port Quin. There is a slightly haunted air about Port Quin today. It is a remote, silent place, yet in 1841 nearly 100 people lived here in a village of over 20 households. Now only a few cottages remain, not all of them occupied permanently. Like most inlets on the North Cornish coast Port Quin survived until the 19th century on pilchard fishing and on coastal trade that involved the import of coal and lime in exchange for slate, and lead from small mining concerns. Legend claims that most of the men of Port Quin were lost at sea in some kind of fishing or smuggling disaster and that the womenfolk and children moved away. There was certainly rapid depopulation, but it may simply have been through emigration when mining failed and pilchard fishing declined in the late 19th century. The route you follow through the fields back to bustling Port Isaac must once have been a local highway between two thriving communities.

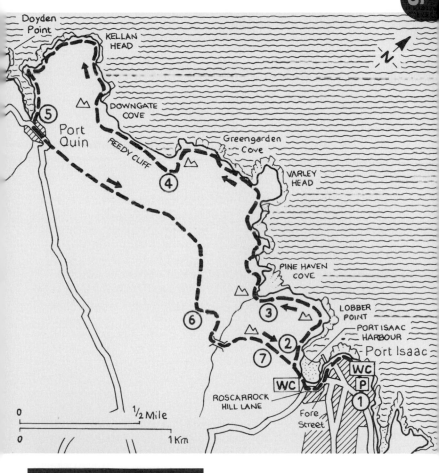

Walk 16 Directions

① Leave the **Port Isaac main car park** by the lower terrace and turn left along a track, keeping right where it branches, signposted

'**Coast Path**'. At the road, keep ahead and down **Fore Street** to reach the open space known as **the Platt** at the entry to the harbour. Just past **Port Isaac Fishermen Ltd**, turn right up **Roscarrock Hill Lane**, signposted '**Coast Path**'.

② At the top of the lane, pass a public footpath sign on the left, then, in 30yds (27m), keep to the right of the gateway to a terrace of houses and bear right, signposted '**Coastal Footpath**'. Follow the path round **Lobber Point**.

③ Descend to **Pine Haven Cove** and go over a wooden stile. (A wooden fence marches alongside the inside edge of the path from here on.) Climb steeply uphill and round the edge of an enormous gulf. Go over a stile at the end of the fenced section and cross **Varley Head**. (The path ahead again runs close to the cliff edge and is fenced on the inside.)

> **WHILE YOU'RE THERE** ⓘ
>
> Take the opportunity to explore Port Isaac. The alleyways of the village reach their most eccentric form in the narrowest of passageways, known as 'drangs', with splendid names such as 'Shuggy's Ope' and 'Squeeze-ee-Belly Alley', the latter speaking for itself. Where Fore Street, at its bottom end, bends sharply round to the harbour, keep ahead along a narrow alley to find these.

④ Just beyond a bench descend steep steps, (there is a hand rail) into **Downgate Cove** and **Reedy Cliff**. Follow the coast path up some very steep sections to reach the seaward edge of **Kellan Head**. Continue along the coast path to **Port Quin**.

⑤ Turn left at Port Quin and go up the road past the car park entrance.

> **WHERE TO EAT AND DRINK** ⓘ
>
> There are no refreshment stops on the route, but Port Isaac has a number of cafés and restaurants. The **Slipway Restaurant**, **Harbour Cafe** and the **Wheelhouse Seafood Restaurant and Bistro** are clustered round the entrance to the harbour beach and the nearby **Golden Lion** does sandwiches and bar meals. The **Old Drug Store**, on the way down Fore Street serves fish and chips.

At a bend in the road bear off left, signposted '**Public Footpath to Port Isaac**'. Go past cottages and keep up the slope to a gate with a stone stile. Dogs should be kept under strict control from here on. Follow the path alongside a hedge, then climb to a stile between two gates. Keep alongside the right-hand edge of the next fields.

⑥ Go over a stile beside a gate, then turn left and follow the left field edge to a wooden stile. Go left over the stile and descend into the wooded valley bottom. Cross a wooden footbridge over a stream, then go over a stone stile. Keep ahead and climb very steeply through gorse to reach an open field slope. Keep ahead across the field (no apparent path), aiming to the left of a tall wooden pole that soon comes into view.

⑦ Cross a stone stile and follow the hedged-in path downhill to a junction with the lane at Point ②. Turn right and retrace your steps to **Port Isaac** and then to the car park.

> **WHAT TO LOOK FOR** ⓘ
>
> The tangled vegetation of the Reedy Cliff area makes an ideal habitat for small birds such as the **stonechat**. This is a typical passerine, or percher. The male bird is easily distinguished by its russet breast, white collar and dark head while the female is a duller brown overall. The 'stonechat' name derives from the bird's distinctive chattering note that resembles a rapid tapping of stone on stone.

Along the Banks of the River Camel at Wadebridge

A gentle walk along the famous old railway trackbed of the Camel Trail and through less-visited woodlands.

•DISTANCE•	6 miles (9.7km)
•MINIMUM TIME•	3hrs 30min
•ASCENT / GRADIENT•	328ft (100m)
•LEVEL OF DIFFICULTY•	
•PATHS•	Farm and forestry tracks and well-surfaced old railway track
•LANDSCAPE•	Wooded riverside
•SUGGESTED MAP•	aqua3 OS Explorer 106 Newquay and Padstow
•START / FINISH•	Grid reference. SW 991722
•DOG FRIENDLINESS•	Dogs should be kept under control and restrained from roaming fields and property adjacent to the Camel Trail. On lead through grazed areas and if notices indicate
•PARKING•	Wadebridge main car park. Small parking area at end of Guineaport Road at start of the Camel Trail
•PUBLIC TOILETS•	The Platt, Wadebridge

BACKGROUND TO THE WALK

Wadebridge is emphatically a river town. Even its name defines it as such. Before the mid-15th century the settlement on the banks of the Camel River, upstream from Padstow was known simply as 'Waed', the fording place. It was a dangerous passage across the Camel here and there were many drownings and near escapes. Eventually, in 1485, money was raised for the building of a bridge, known subsequently as 'The Bridge on Wool'. Contemporary records suggest that the foundations for the stone piers of the new bridge were actually made up of wool sacks. But another, less appealing but possibly more accurate, explanation is that the money for the bridge was earned from the lucrative wool trade of the medieval period. The bridge has 17 arches and is 320ft (98m) long. It was widened in 1847 and is recognised as being one of the finest examples of a medieval bridge in Britain.

Famous Railway

In the 19th century Wadebridge also acquired a famous railway, first linking the town to Bodmin in 1834 and then to Padstow in 1899. The Wadebridge to Bodmin section was built to carry sand extracted from the Camel Estuary for agricultural use to improve soil conditions. In return the railway carried china clay and granite from the quarries on Bodmin Moor for export by sea. Extending the railway line to Padstow led to the decline of Wadebridge as a port but the Padstow link also established the line as part of the great Atlantic Coast Express carrying huge numbers of holidaymakers from London and the heart of England to the Cornish seaside resorts. The journey from Bodmin through Wadebridge to Padstow was immortalised by the poet John Betjeman who described its length as 'the most beautiful train journey...'

Recreational Trail

The line was closed in the 1960s. In 1980 Cornwall County Council bought the section from Boscarne Junction near Bodmin to Padstow and turned it into a recreational trail, the Camel Trail, that has subsequently been enjoyed by vast numbers of walkers, cyclists, horse riders, anglers and birdwatchers. This walk follows part of the Camel Trail, but first leads inland through deeply wooded countryside. The route climbs steadily above the Camel valley to the serene little hamlet of Burlawn before it descends into an enfolding blanket of woodland by Hustyn Mill from where it leads to Polbrock Bridge, where the River Camel and the Camel Trail cling to each other like snakes. From Polbrock Bridge you follow the Camel Trail effortlessly back to Wadebridge, in more crowded circumstances at times and sharing the experience with cyclists, yet within that same persuasive world of trees, river, and Cornish air that so enchanted Betjeman.

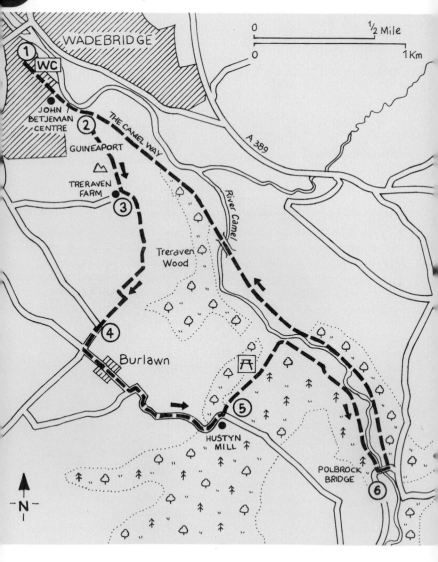

Walk 17 ‖ **Directions**

① From the car parks in Wadebridge, walk along **Southern Way Road** past the **Betjeman Centre** and continue along **Guineaport Road** to the start of the **Camel Trail**. Start from here if adjacent parking is used.

> **WHERE TO EAT AND DRINK** ⓘ
>
> There are no refreshment outlets along the route but Wadebridge has a number of pubs, restaurants and cafés. The **Swan Hotel** in Molesworth Street, the town's main street leading to its famous bridge, does good traditional food.

② Do not follow the Camel Trail. Instead, where the road forks just past a row of houses, keep right and within a few paces, at a junction, where the road curves up to the right, keep ahead along an unsurfaced track signposted '**Public Footpath to Treraven**'. Follow the track steadily uphill. Go through a wooden gate and follow the right-hand field edge to go through another gate. Continue along a track to reach a junction with a wider track. Keep ahead and follow the track.

> **WHILE YOU'RE THERE** ⓘ
>
> Visit the **John Betjeman Centre** in Southern Way, Wadebridge. It's in the old railway station and contains memorabilia of the famous Poet Laureate. He was unsurpassed as a chronicler of suburbia and the countryside, and a lover of the Padstow and Wadebridge area where he had a family home. Open Monday to Friday, 10–4:30.

③ Go left in front of **Treraven Farm**, then, in about 15yds (14m), at a junction, keep right and continue along the track to reach a bend on a minor public road by a building.

④ Keep straight ahead along the road, with care, then turn left at a cross roads, signposted '**Burlawn**'. At the next junction, go left and follow the road through Burlawn. Go steeply downhill on a narrow lane overshadowed by trees.

⑤ At **Hustyn Mill**, beyond a little footbridge, turn left off the road and follow a broad woodland track. Stay on the main track to where it reaches the surfaced road at **Polbrock Bridge**.

> **WHAT TO LOOK FOR** ⓘ
>
> The River Camel and its flanking woods are a perfect habitat for birds. Look for goldfinch and nuthatch, amongst the trees and for heron and curlew on the river. In the spring and autumn, if you are very lucky, you may spot birds of passage such as the beautiful little egret in its snow-white plumage.

⑥ Turn left over the bridge across the **River Camel** and, in a few paces, go off left and down steps to join the **Camel Trail**. Turn left here and follow the unwavering line of the Camel Trail back to **Wadebridge**.

Walk 17

The World of Daphne du Maurier at Fowey

Exploring the coast and countryside near Fowey where the novelist Daphne du Maurier found inspiration for her romantic novels.

•DISTANCE•	7½ miles (12km)
•MINIMUM TIME•	4hrs
•ASCENT / GRADIENT•	820ft (250m) ▲▲▲
•LEVEL OF DIFFICULTY•	🚶🚶 🚶🚶 🚶
•PATHS•	Field paths, rough lanes and coastal footpath, can be very muddy on inland tracks during wet weather, 12 stiles
•LANDSCAPE•	Coastal fields, woodland and open coastal cliffs.
•SUGGESTED MAP•	aqua3 OS Explorer 107 St Austell & Liskeard
•START / FINISH•	Grid reference: SX 118511
•DOG FRIENDLINESS•	Dogs on lead through grazed areas. No dogs allowed on Polkerris Beach, Easter to Oct 31
•PARKING•	Readymoney Cove car park, reached by continuing on from entrance to Fowey's main car park
•PUBLIC TOILETS•	Readymoney Cove and Polkerris

BACKGROUND TO THE WALK

Fowey and its environs cry out for the romantic novel and it is no surprise that the area inspired the writer Daphne du Maurier, who for many years lived as a favoured tenant at Menabilly House, the ancestral home of the Rashleigh family. The house and its environs became embedded in her work. Menabilly was the shadowy inspiration for the fictional house of 'Manderley' in du Maurier's compelling work *Rebecca*. The house also inspired the setting for *My Cousin Rachel*. If you are a fan of du Maurier, you may take special pleasure in this walk. If you are not a fan, then you may soon become one.

Love Lane

The walk starts from the charmingly named Readymoney Cove, a corrupted form of the Cornish *redeman*, possibly translating as 'stony ford'. From the cove you follow Love Lane, a very old cart way that rises over scarred rock slabs into the shrouding trees of Covington Wood. Soon open fields are reached and the route strikes inland along field paths and enclosed tracks. In the little valley below Lankelly Farm the path passes through a tunnel and beneath what was once a carriageway leading to Menabilly House. Beyond Tregaminion Farm and church the long western flank of the Gribbin Peninsula is reached. Here you can divert down a zig-zag path to Polkerris Cove and beach (► While You're There).

The coastal footpath is followed south to Gribbin Head and its crowning 'Daymark', an immense Graeco-Gothic edifice erected in 1832 as a warning mark to sailors who too often had mistaken the shallow waters of St Austell Bay for the secure anchorage of Falmouth Roads further west. The Daymark was erected on land granted by William Rashleigh of Menabilly. The inscription rather neatly defines the mercantile priorities of the day, the 'safety of commerce' first, 'preservation of mariners' second. Now, the Daymark, and its garish red and white stripes, is forgiven for its naked intrusion because of its historical significance. Head north from here to Polridmouth Cove (P'ridmouth to the initiated) and the heart of 'du Maurier Country', from where a minor roller coaster hike takes you to St Catherine's Point and to the ruins of the 16th-century St Catherine's Castle. The castle was part of a chain of defences built on the orders of Henry VIII as a precaution against potential invasion from France. Its lower level housed later 18th-century guns. From the high ground of St Catherine's Point there is a steep descent to Readymoney Cove.

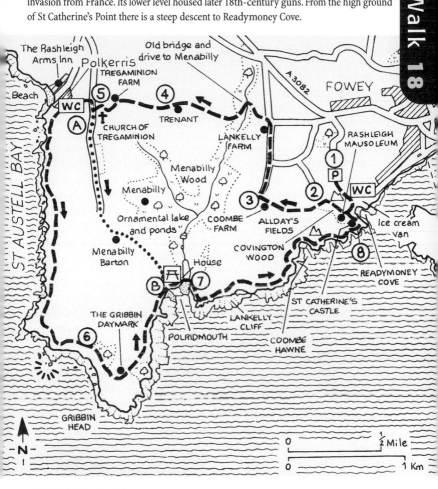

Walk 18 Directions

① From the bottom end of the car park walk down **St Catherine's Parade**, then turn right towards the inlet of **Readymoney Cove**. Continue to the end of the road, above the beach and follow the initially rocky **Love Lane** uphill on the Saints Way. Carry on past the

first junction, ignoring the options by a National Trust sign for 'Covington Woods'.

② Turn left at the next junction and climb wooden steps to reach **Allday's Fields**. Follow the right-hand field edge. At a field gap follow an obvious grassy track ahead to a lane end at **Coombe Farm**. Follow the lane ahead.

Walk 18

③ At a road, turn right and continue to **Lankelly Farm**. Pass a junction on the right and follow **Prickly Post Lane** for a few paces. Turn off left onto a gravel drive, then keep left and along a narrow fenced-in path.

④ Go up a wide, rough track by derelict buildings at **Trenant**, then go over a stile on the left. Keep ahead alongside the field edge, then follow the path to a stile into a field below **Tregaminion Farm**. Go up the field to a gate, continue between buildings then turn right, then left, to reach a T-junction with a road by the entrance gate to the little **Church of Tregaminion**.

> ### WHILE YOU'RE THERE ⓘ
> Visit **Polkerris**, the small cove and beach tucked in the eastern arm of St Austell Bay. It was once a busy fishing village in the days when the great bight of St Austell Bay saw vast shoals of pilchard staining its clear waters purple. Today Polkerris and the green flank of the Gribbin Peninsula stand as a counter image to the industrial landscape of the bay's opposite shore where the work buildings of the china clay industry stumble across the skyline.

⑤ Turn right and in 100yds (91m) go left into a field. Reach a junction on the edge of some woods. (An enjoyable diversion is to take the right-hand branch leading to the beach and cove at **Polkerris**.) On the main route, keep left along the

> ### WHERE TO EAT AND DRINK ⓘ
> There is usually an ice cream and soft drinks van at Readymoney Cove during the summer months. It is worth making the diversion into the little harbourside village of Polkerris where the **Rashleigh Inn** overlooks the beach and offers reasonable pub lunches. The **Lifeboat House beach shop,** opposite the Rashleigh Inn, does Cornish pasties and sandwiches to take away.

field edge and follow the well-defined coast path for 1¼ miles (2km) to **Gribbin Head**.

⑥ Enter the wooded National Trust property of the **Gribbin**. Keep left at a junction. Go through a gate and cross to the **Gribbin Daymark**. Go left and down a faint grassy track, then follow the coast path to **Polridmouth**.

⑦ Follow the coast path, signposted '**Lankelly Cliff**'. At open ground, follow the seaward field edge. Go steeply in to, and out of, **Coombe Hawne**. Enter **Covington Wood**, keep left at the immediate junction, and pass the **Rashleigh Mausoleum**.

⑧ Turn right at a junction to reach **St Catherine's Castle**. Return along the path then go down steps at the first junction on the right. Go down wooden steps to **Readymoney Beach**. Return to the car park via **St Catherine's Parade**.

> ### WHAT TO LOOK FOR ⓘ
> Along the vegetated borders of the fields and woods look for the tall pinkish flower spike of rosebay willowherb. This tall plant with its purple flowers, that give way to cottony seeds in autumn, was once rare in Britain. It is thought that it spread rapidly throughout the country with the coming of the railways in the 19th century. The frequent scorching of embankments from stray sparks during the old days of steam trains created ideal growing conditions for the willowherb's windblown seeds. The web of railway lines also served as a disseminator for many other plants. Look for the madly tangled and trailing blooms of great bindweed, with their white flowerheads.

Polridmouth Cove and the Menabilly Estate

A shorter walk on the estate lands of Daphne du Maurier Country.
See map and information panel for Walk 18

•DISTANCE•	5 miles (8km)
•MINIMUM TIME•	3hrs
•ASCENT / GRADIENT•	656ft (200m) ▲▲▲
•LEVEL OF DIFFICULTY•	秋 秋 秋

Walk 19 Directions
(Walk 18 option)

This shortened version of Walk 18 allows more time to enjoy **Polridmouth Cove**. You can also make a short diversion south to visit the **Gribbin Daymark**. Follow the main walk as far as Point ⑤ from where you turn left along the road. At a car park, continue along the surfaced road, signposted '**Menabilly Farm**'. Continue when the surfaced road becomes a track, and then a path, that descends to **Polridmouth Cove.**

The farm at **Menabilly Barton** was the home farm of the Rashleigh family's Menabilly Estate and it was here that Daphne du Maurier was said to have been inspired to write her classic horror story *The Birds* by the sight of ravenous gulls following the plough. The story became the basis of the famous Alfred Hitchcock film portraying a world overpowered by murderous feathered flocks. You will see plenty of gulls on this walk, screeching and wheeling, but, vivid imagination apart, be assured that there is no record of bird attacks in the area.

There has been a problem created in recent times by the increasing amount of accessible domestic rubbish and the random feeding of gulls by visitors in seaside resorts, producing a breed of audacious scavengers. Perhaps the story is not so far fetched.

Polridmouth Cove was used by du Maurier as the setting for the death of the eponymous heroine of *Rebecca*. Today Polridmouth retains much of its picturesque character. The lake was created in the early 20th century as a pleasant adjunct to the Menabilly Estate. The house by the lake stands on the site of an old corn mill. Polridmouth's lake was made use of during the Second World War as a night-time decoy in a bid to protect the strategically important Fowey Harbour. Illuminations, remotely controlled to seem like carelessly exposed harbour and building lights, were placed round the lake and smaller, adjoining ponds. A rigidly-enforced blackout kept Fowey in total darkness. Luckily for both, no bombs fell in the area and Polridmouth survives today with its ornamental lake intact, still striking a happy contrast with the wild foreshore.

Padstow Perambulation

A short stroll through the oldest part of Padstow followed by a walk alongside the Camel Estuary.

•DISTANCE•	3 miles (4.8km)
•MINIMUM TIME•	2hrs 30min
•ASCENT / GRADIENT•	197ft (60m) ▲▲ ▲▲ ▲▲
•LEVEL OF DIFFICULTY•	🚶 🚶 🚶
•PATHS•	Surfaced walkways, coastal footpath and country lane, 2 stiles
•LANDSCAPE•	Traditional fishing village and estuary shoreline
•SUGGESTED MAP•	aqua3 OS Explorer 106 Newquay and Padstow
•START / FINISH•	Grid reference: SW 917753
•DOG FRIENDLINESS•	Dogs on lead through grazed areas. Dogs on leads are welcomed in the grounds of Prideaux Place
•PARKING•	Padstow main car park on outskirts of village. Car park at Padstow Harbour and old railway station
•PUBLIC TOILETS•	Main and harbour car parks. The Strand, Padstow Harbour

Walk 20 Directions

The North Cornish port of Padstow takes its old name of 'Petroc's Stow' from Cornwall's patron saint St Petroc. Padstow is a delightful town and is particularly famous for its May Day festival of the 'Obby Oss', during which symbolic hobby horses, made of great hooped masks with trailing black skirts, are danced round the streets in celebration of ancient fertility rites. It is an unforgettable experience, although attempting a quiet stroll, like the one described here, is perhaps best left for any other day of the year than May Day.

If you have parked at the town's main car park, leave from the bottom right-hand corner, to the left of a toilet block. Go down to a junction with a surfaced walkway and turn left. (If you park in the lower car park, leave by steps at the

bottom of the car park and turn left along the walkway.) Follow the walkway to reach the churchyard of **St Petroc's Church**, (► While You're There). Turn left, facing the church porch, and walk through the churchyard between tall cypresses. Go through a metal gate into **Church Street**, opposite the charming **Poppy Cottage,** then turn left and walk up to a junction with **Tregirls Lane**. Turn right and then go right again into **High Street**. The houses and buildings in this part of Padstow feature some of the town's finest vernacular architecture.

WHAT TO LOOK FOR ℹ

Along the banks of the Camel Estuary, at Gun Point and above the dunes, look for maritime plants such as early scurvy grass, with its glossy leaves and pink flowers, the red-tinged sea beet and the deep-rooted sea rocket, a straggling plant with green fleshy leaves and pale lilac flowers. Look for Coltsfoot too with its yellow daisy-like head and a silvery stem.

Just before **High Street**'s junction with **Cross Street** and **Fentonluna Lane**, go right into a fascinating passageway called **Marble Arch**. Watch your head at low sections as you pass through to reach steps that lead down into **Church Street** once more. Turn left here and join **Duke Street** at a junction with **Cross Street**. Walk down the raised terrace of **Duke Street** and, where the terrace ends, cross over and go right along **Middle Street**, passing the attractive Victorian almshouses on the left. There are some fine galleries and craft shops in Middle Street. At the end of Middle Street, turn into **Lanadwell Street**, passing the **Golden Lion Inn** and then the **London Inn** with its handsome timber-framed façade in red brick and slate. In summer the whole inn is a veritable hanging garden of colourful flowers. At the end of Lanadwell Street reach **Broad Street**. Turn left here and walk along the busy **Market Place** then on down an alleyway past the impressive building of the **Old Ship Inn**, to emerge at the **Strand** and the **Harbour**.

WHILE YOU'RE THERE i

The **Church of St Petroc** is a substantial building with a broad nave and aisles and fine wagon roofs and artefacts, including a splendid font in Cataclews stone from Cataclews Point at nearby Harlyn Bay. St Petroc's has a pleasing gloominess created by its darkly shrouding trees and by the dark mossy slate of its walls and tower. At the end of the described route is the splendid **Prideaux Place**, an Elizabethan house that has been lived in by the Prideaux-Brune family for over 400 years. There are guided tours of the house and its sumptuously furnished rooms. The landscaped gardens are also open to the public. Open Easter, and late May to September, Sunday–Thursday, 1·30–5.

The next section of the walk takes you alongside the estuary of the **River Camel**. Walk along the harbour's **North Quay** past **Abbey House**, a distinctive medieval building, slate hung and with an open mullion window below which is a stone head in a niche. Continue to where the road forks, just past the **tourist information centre**.

WHERE TO EAT AND DRINK i

In Padstow you really are spoilt for choice when it comes to the finest Cornish cuisine. The celebrity chef **Rick Stein** has a number of establishments in the town and these are more than matched by other fine restaurants and a host of food outlets at all levels. The town also boasts a number of excellent pubs and traditional inns. There are no food outlets on the estuary section of the walk but Prideaux Place has the very pleasant **Terrace Tea Rooms**.

Keep left here and uphill, signposted '**Coast Path**' and '**To Lower Beach**'. Follow the walkway through **Chapel Style Field** and on to a war memorial at **St Saviour's Point** and then to **St George's Cove** and **Gun Point**. Continue along the path above an area of sand dunes, then reach a stile into a field. Follow the field edge to a T-junction with a stony track and turn left and uphill to **Tregirls Farm**. Follow the surfaced lane from in front of the farm for about ⅓ mile (536m), then pass beneath an archway and reach the Elizabethan building of **Prideaux Place** (➤ While You're There). Continue to the end of Tregirls Lane and then turn left down **Church Street**. Opposite **Poppy Cottage** go through the churchyard gate and retrace your steps to the car park. Alternatively you can continue down **Church Street** and back to **Padstow Harbour**.

Ancient Walls on the Lonely Dodman

A circuit of the headland of Dodman Point, where Iron Age people established a fortified encampment.

•DISTANCE•	4½ miles (7.2km)
•MINIMUM TIME•	3hrs
•ASCENT / GRADIENT•	377ft (115m) ▲▲▲
•LEVEL OF DIFFICULTY•	🚶 🚶 🚶
•PATHS•	Good coastal paths. Inland paths can be muddy, 9 stiles
•LANDSCAPE•	Open fields and coastal cliffs
•SUGGESTED MAP•	aqua3 OS Explorer 105 Falmouth & Mevagissey
•START / FINISH•	Grid reference: SX 011415
•DOG FRIENDLINESS•	Dogs on lead through grazed areas
•PARKING•	Gorran Haven car park, pay at kiosk
•PUBLIC TOILETS•	Gorran Haven

BACKGROUND TO THE WALK

The high and lonely headland of Dodman Point thrusts its great bulk into the sea near Mevagissey and Gorran Haven, forming the eastern arch of Veryan Bay, on the south coast of Cornwall. Local people make no bones about the name. To them this dark and brooding promontory has always been the 'Deadman'. It was recorded as such on old maps. The source of the name may be prosaic, of course, a probable distortion of an ancient Cornish word; but 'Deadman' strikes a suitably menacing echo with the nearby Vault Beach and with the threatening names of such tideline rocks as the Bell and Mean-lay that lie at the base of the 328ft (100m) Dodman cliffs. By whatever name, the Dodman is a natural fortress, and across its broad shoulders lies a massive earthen embankment, the landward defences of a 'promontory fort'. This is one of a number of such protected farm settlements that dates back to the Cornish Iron Age.

Vault Beach
The first part of the walk leads from the village of Gorran Haven along the coastal footpath to the great sweep of Vault Beach, or Bow Beach, as it is also known. From above the beach the path rises steadily to the broad-backed promontory of the Dodman. The headland is crowned with a sepulchral granite cross placed there in 1896 by the Reverend George Martin, Rector of nearby St Michael Caerhays. Whether or not the cross was placed as a navigation aid or as a religious gesture is not entirely clear. The inscription on the cross argues for Martin's religious certainties above all. Just inland from the cross (➤ Directions Point ④), but hidden by scrub, is the Dodman Watch House, a charming survivor of the late 18th century. This much restored little building was an Admiralty signal station, part of a chain of similar structures along the English Channel Coast. It was used in later years by coastguards and has been restored by the National Trust.

From the Dodman, the route follows the coast path for a short distance along the headland's western flank to where a gate allows access to fields that bear the vestigial marks of prehistoric and medieval cultivation systems. On the main route, you turn off the coast path here to follow the line of a great Iron Age earthwork, known as the Bulwark. This is an impressive piece of engineering, even by today's standards, some 2,000ft (609 m) in length and over 12ft (4m) high. Eventually a track leads to the serene hamlet of Penare and then across fields and down a little valley back into Gorran Haven.

Walk 21 Directions

① Turn left on leaving the car park and walk down to **Gorran Haven** harbour. Just before the access to the beach, turn right up **Fox Hole Lane**, then go up steps, signposted 'Vault Beach'. Go up more steps, and then through a gate. Follow the coast path ahead, past a sign for the National Trust property of **Lamledra**.

② Keep left at a junction below a rocky outcrop. A steep alternative path leads up right from here, past a memorial plaque, to rejoin the main coast path. On the main route however go down some stone steps and follow the path along the slope. At a junction, keep right. The left-hand track at this junction leads down to **Vault Beach** from where you can regain the coastal path by another track leading uphill. Keep left at the next junction.

Walk 21

③ Go left over a stile and follow a path through scrubland. Keep ahead at a junction signed '**Dodman Point**' then go over a stile onto open ground. Continue on this footpath to the summit of Dodman Point.

④ As you approach the large granite cross on the summit of the Dodman, reach a first junction from where a path going right leads to the **Watch House**. Continue towards the cross on the summit and then, just before the cross and at the next junction and arrow post, go right along the coast path.

⑤ Go over a stile beyond a gate with an access notice pinned to it. Reach a junction in a few paces. Turn right and follow the path between the high banks of the **Bulwark**.

⑥ Keep ahead where a path comes in from the right. Follow the hedged track to reach a kissing gate and a surfaced lane at **Penare**. Turn right along the lane.

⑦ At a junction leave the road and go through a field gate signposted '**Treveague**'. Keep across two fields, then at a road end by houses, turn right, signposted '**Gorran Haven**'. Go left at another signpost and go along a drive behind a house, bearing round right. Go left through a gate and then along a path above a small valley.

⑧ Cross a muddy area by some stepping stones, then go through a gate. Follow the driveway ahead to a T-junction with the public road. Turn right and walk down, with care as there can be traffic, to **Gorran Haven** car park.

Giant Steps and Staircases at Bedruthan

Exploring the spectacular coastal landscape at Bedruthan Steps and Park Head.

•DISTANCE•	4½ miles (7.2km)
•MINIMUM TIME•	2hrs 30min
•ASCENT / GRADIENT•	131ft (40m) ▲▲ ▲
•LEVEL OF DIFFICULTY•	👥 👥 👥
•PATHS•	Coastal paths and field paths. Coast path very close to unguarded cliff edges in some places. Take care in windy weather and with children and dogs. 1 stile
•LANDSCAPE•	Spectacular cliffs and dramatic sea stacks
•SUGGESTED MAP•	aqua3 OS Explorer 106 Newquay and Padstow
•START / FINISH•	Grid reference: SW 850691
•DOG FRIENDLINESS•	Dogs on lead through grazed areas
•PARKING•	National Trust car park at Carnewas. Or at the National Trust Park Head car park, grid reference: SW 851706, from where the walk can also be started at Point ⑤
•PUBLIC TOILETS•	Carnewas car park

BACKGROUND TO THE WALK

The flat, unremarkable countryside that lies inland from Bedruthan Steps belies the stupendous nature of the area's coastline. Green fields run to the sliced-off edges of 300ft (90m) cliffs. At the foot of the cliffs lie dramatic rock islands that at high tide are besieged by crashing waves and at low tide, spring from a smooth expanse of golden, sea-damp sand. This was Victorian 'picturesque' at its most melodramatic and the area was popular with 'excursionists' in the late 19th century. The islands, or stacks, are portrayed as being the stepping stones of a legendary giant called Bedruthan, but this conceit blew in with the first of the Victorian tourists. The stacks acquired picturesque names such as 'The Queen Bess Rock', which, before losing its head to erosion, was said to resemble the figure of Elizabeth I, who never lost her head in any sense.

Miners

For many years, before tourists and tall tales of giants, there were flights of steps cut into the cliff faces below Carnewas and further north at Pentire in the crook of coastline south of Park Head. These staircases were known as Carnewas Steps and Pentire Steps and were probably used by local people to collect seaweed and to land cargoes, legitimate or otherwise. Miners may also have sought access to the beach. There was 19th-century mining at Carnewas – the National Trust shop and tearoom are housed in old mine buildings – and tin, copper and lead may have originally been extracted from tunnels, known as adits, at the base of the cliffs.

Today you can reach Bedruthan Beach down a secure staircase reached from the coast path, part way along the route of the walk from the start at Carnewas car park. A descent of the beach staircase is worthwhile, (▶ While You're There). From the top of the steps the coast path leads north towards Park Head passing on the way, the vestigial remains of Redcliff Castle, an Iron Age fortified settlement whose landward embankments are all that remain of a protruding headland long since collapsed into the sea. From beyond Redcliff Castle, one of the finest views of Bedruthan Beach can be had; but do not go too close to the cliff edge. The circuit of Park Head, via the pleasant cove of Porth Mear, rounds off the walk. You can walk out to the promontory of Park Head itself passing through the defensive banks of another Iron Age fortified settlement across the neck of the headland. From here the coast path leads back past Redcliff Castle and then to Carnewas.

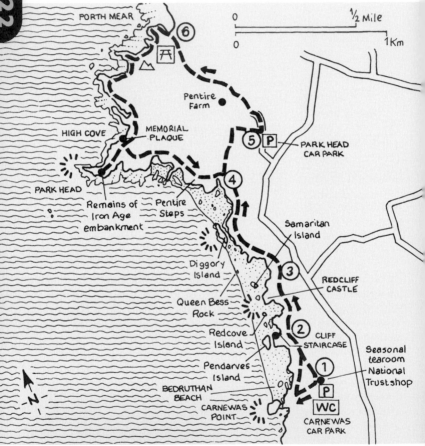

Walk 22 Directions

① From **Carnewas car park**, go through a gap in the wall on the right of the National Trust shop, then, in a few paces, bear off to the left at a junction. Follow the path to a crossing of paths and go straight across and down a grassy path to the dramatic view from **Carnewas Point** of **Bedruthan Beach** and the sea stacks. Return to the crossing and follow a path left along the cliff edge. (Take note of warning notices.) At a junction with a cobbled path, go left and descend to a dip at **Pendarves Point**.

Walk 22

WHAT TO LOOK FOR ℹ

At low water on the beach watch out for turnstones, brisk little birds with chestnut and black and white plumage and small heads. They dash across the damp sand 'turning' over stones in search of tiny shellfish and sandhoppers. Along the tops of the cliffs watch also for the silent, unflappable flight of the stubby-winged fulmar. This remarkable seabird was once found only in far northern waters and is believed to have spread south by following herring fishing boats returning to their English ports. The first fulmar to be identified in Cornish waters was spotted by fishermen during the 1930s. The fulmar has two small holes on its upper beak through which it ejects a foul-smelling green liquid at predators. Don't get too close.

② At a junction in the dip, go down left to reach the top of the cliff staircase. On re-ascending the staircase, go back uphill to the junction with the coast path and turn left past a National Trust sign for '**Carnewas**'. Follow the coast path alongside a wooden fence and below a parking area with picnic tables above.

③ Pass **Redcliff Castle**, then, where the path forks by a signpost, follow either fork to where they rejoin. Keep to the right of a stone wall, that has tamarisk trees sprouting from it, to reach a wooden kissing gate. Continue along the open clifftop to reach a set of wooden gates on the right.

④ Go right and through the smaller gate, then follow a permissive footpath along field

WHERE TO EAT AND DRINK ℹ

There are no refreshment opportunities on the route, but there is a **National Trust Tearoom** at Carnewas car park. Open in summer, 10:30–5:30.

edges. Just before the buildings at **Pentire**, turn right through a gate and follow field edges to reach **Parkhead car park**.

⑤ Turn left and go left down a surfaced lane. Just before the **Pentire** buildings go through a gate on the right, signposted '**Porthmear Beach and Park Head**'. Bear left across the field to a stile and gateway. Bear right down the next field to a wooden kissing gate in its bottom corner. Go through the gate and follow a path through a wetland area to join the coast path above the attractive **Porth Mear**.

WHILE YOU'RE THERE ℹ

A descent of the **cliff staircase** to **Bedruthan Beach** should not be missed as part of this walk, if you feel fit enough. The steps have been ably secured by the National Trust and are protected from the risk of falling stones by vast swathes of wire netting fixed to the beetling cliff faces above. The steps are steep and there are 139 of them – or thereabouts. Be careful on the rocky foreshore where the rock can be very slippery. At low tide you can explore the beach, but be very aware of tide times; the flooding tide can cut you off very quickly. The day's tide times are usually displayed at the top of the steps. You are not advised to swim from Bedruthan Beach. The staircase is closed to the public November–February.

⑥ Go left and follow the coast path steadily uphill and then round **Park Head**. Take care when close to the cliff edges. At a memorial plaque above **High Cove**, divert to the promontory of Park Head itself. Return to the plaque and follow the coast path south to Point ④. Retrace your steps to Point ②, in the dip above the start of the cliff staircase. Follow the cobbled walkway uphill and back to **Carnewas car park**.

Hidden Cornwall at Nare Head

A coastal and field walk through some of South Cornwall's more remote and endearing landscapes.

•DISTANCE•	7 miles (11.3km)
•MINIMUM TIME•	5hrs
•ASCENT / GRADIENT•	1,312ft (400m) ▲▲ ▲▲ ▲
•LEVEL OF DIFFICULTY•	🚶 🚶 🚶
•PATHS•	Good coastal footpath, field paths and quiet lanes. Field stiles are often overgrown, 30 stiles
•LANDSCAPE•	Vegetated coast with some cliffs. Mainly flat fields on inland section
•SUGGESTED MAP•	aqua3 OS Explorer 105 Falmouth & Mevagissey
•START / FINISH•	Grid reference: SW 906384
•DOG FRIENDLINESS•	Dogs on lead through grazed areas
•PARKING•	Carne Beach Car Park. Large National Trust car park behind beach
•PUBLIC TOILETS•	Carne Beach, Portloe, Veryan

BACKGROUND TO THE WALK

There are parts of the Cornish coast that seem especially remote, where main roads have been kept at arms' length and where human development has not gone beyond farming and small scale sea-going. The lonely stretch of South Cornish coast between Gerrans Bay and Veryan Bay, with Nare Head at its centre, is one such place, a landscape where people seem to have lived always at a healthy distance from too much intrusion.

Paradoe
The walk begins at the seasonally popular Carne Beach. A steady hike along the coast path from here soon brings you to a steep descent into the narrow Paradoe, pronounced 'Perada', Cove. On a spur of land above the sea is the ruin of a small cottage. This was the home of a 19th-century fisherman called Mallet , who lived during the week in this lonely spot, fishing from 'Mallet's Cove' below, then returning at weekends to his wife at the village of Veryan, a few miles (kilometres) inland. Eventually Mallet emigrated to Australia – without his wife. Weekends had become non-negotiable, perhaps. The little ruined cottage above the restless sea still speaks of a life of extraordinary detachment.

Portloe
From Paradoe it is a long, punishing climb to the flat top of Nare Head. Beyond the Head a pleasant ramble takes you along the coast past the steep Rosen Cliff and by lonely coves. Offshore lies the formidable Gull Rock (► What to Look For) The route leads to Portloe, a fishing village that seems to have survived without imposed 'quaintness' and without too much intrusion. Here, a steep-sided valley has left only enough room at its seaward end for fishing boats and a pleasant veneer of houses and cottages to either side. You head inland

from this reassuring place into a lost world of little fields and meadows that straggle across country to Veryan (➤ While You're There).

Ancient Landmark

From Veryan the route wanders back towards the sea, past the ancient landmark of Carne Beacon, a Bronze Age burial site that saw later service as a signal station, a triangulation point and as a Second World War observation post. Before these latter uses the bones beneath had been disturbed by curious Victorians. A few fields away lies 'Veryan Castle', known also as 'The Ringarounds', the site of a Late Iron Age farming settlement (➤ Walk 24). These ancient sites prove that this absorbing landscape has given refuge to people for thousands of years. From the high ground the route leads down to the coast once more.

Walk 23 Directions

① Turn left out of the car park and walk up the road, with care. Just past the steep bend, turn off right and go up steps and onto the coast

path. Follow the coast path to **Paradoe Cove** and and continue past **Nare Head**.

② Above **Kiberick Cove** go through a gap in a wall (Walk 24 starts here). For the main route keep ahead through a dip to reach a stile. Follow the coast path to **Portloe**. Go left up the road from the cove, past the **Ship Inn**.

③ Just after a sharp left-hand bend, and where the road narrows, go over a high step stile on the right. Cross a field to a stile, then follow the next field edge. Pass a gate, then, in a few paces, go right and over a stile. Cross the next field to a stile into a lane.

④ Go right along the road past **Camels Farm** for 200yds (183m), then go left over a stile and follow the field edge to another stile. Follow the next field edge, then just before the field corner, go right over a stile. Turn left through a gap, then go diagonally right across the next two fields to a stile. At a road junction, go along the road signposted 'Carne and Pendower'.

⑤ Just past **Tregamenna Manor Farm**, on a bend, go over a stile by a gate. Cut across the corner of the field, then go right over a stile. Cross the next field to a stile and then continue to a T-junction with a lane. (Turn right to visit **Veryan**.)

WHILE YOU'RE THERE ⓘ

Divert from the main route to visit **Veryan**, one of South Cornwall's most fascinating villages. It is famous for its five whitewashed round houses with thatched conical roofs, They date from the early 19th century and were the inspiration of the Revd Jeremiah Trist, a local landowner. Various fanciful myths attach to these houses but they seem to have simply reflected a contemporary fashion for ornamental architecture. Visit Veryan's **Church of St Symphorian**, essentially a Victorian restoration of a previous church.

WHERE TO EAT AND DRINK ⓘ

An ice cream and soft drinks van operates at Carne Beach during the summer. The **Tregain Tea Room** and licensed restaurant, just up from the harbour at Portloe is a delight. It offers morning coffee, lunches and special dishes on Sundays. Portloe's **Ship Inn** is a pleasant pub with a large beer garden and a good selection of pub food. At Veryan, the **New Inn** has a good selection of spicy and traditional food. Opposite is the friendly **Tregarthen Coffee Shop**, part of Elerkey Guest House, offering morning coffees, afternoon teas and delicious Cornish cream teas.

---

⑥ If you're not visiting Veryan village, turn left, then, just past **Churchtown Farm**, go left again over a stile. Follow the edge of the field to a stile into a lane. Go immediately left over two stiles, then follow a path, past **Carne Beacon**, to a lane.

⑦ At a corner junction keep ahead down the lane, signposted 'Carne Village Only'. Bear right down a driveway past **Beacon Cottage**. Go through the gate signposted '**Defined Footpaths Nos 44 & 45**'. Follow the track round to the right between a garage and house, then follow a grassy track, keeping ahead at a junction signposted 'Carne Beach'. Go through a gate (put dogs on leads here please) and follow a path alongside a grassy bank and fence.

⑧ Abreast of an old wooden gate up on the right, bear away left and downhill through the scrub, (the path isn't evident at first), and soon pick up a path that leads through gorse to join the coast path back to **Carne Beach** and the car park.

Kiberick Cove, Veryan Castle and Carne

Using special National Trust access paths to explore the coastal hinterland.
See map and information panel for Walk 23

•DISTANCE•	5 miles (8km)
•MINIMUM TIME•	3hrs 30min
•ASCENT / GRADIENT•	459ft (140m) ▲▲ ▲▲ ▲
•LEVEL OF DIFFICULTY•	👫 👫 👫

Walk 24 Directions (Walk 23 option)

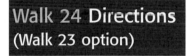

The key to this shortened version of Walk 23 is a path, established by the National Trust, that leads from the coast at Point ②, above **Kiberick Cove**, to a National Trust car park. Step through the gap in the wall at Point ②, then turn sharply left and follow a path uphill and round to the right to reach a stile into a lane end at Point Ⓐ. Turn right and follow the lane inland to reach a right-hand bend just past a house. Go left and over a stile here, follow the left edge of a field, then go over another stile on the left. Cross the next field to reach a gate, go through the gate, then turn right and follow the right-hand field edge to reach a stile into a road at Point Ⓑ. Turn left here and follow Walk 23 to Point ⑤ and onward.

The area to the south of **Veryan** contains not only the Bronze Age **Carne Beacon**, but also 'Veryan Castle', site of an Iron Age settlement. The name is a much later creation but this was probably a protected farmstead, in use before, during and after the Roman

occupation of southern Britain. The site is now in the care of the National Trust, which has established an access route along permissive paths. You can visit it by diverting from the route of this walk at Point Ⓒ. Turn right along the lane to reach the access path to Veryan Castle on the left. A path can also be followed from the Castle back down to the car park at Carne Beach. This makes an interesting alternative to returning to the route of Walk 23 through **Carne** hamlet at Point ⑦.

WHAT TO LOOK FOR ⓘ

Gull Rock, the steep-sided island that lies a short distance offshore from Nare Head is a seabird colony. It has belonged to the National Trust since 1989. The Rock's seabirds were exploited for centuries; their eggs were harvested for food, a precarious exercise because the bulk of seabirds nest on the sheer, land-facing cliff. The birds themselves were also trapped and shot for food. In its time Gull Rock even featured as a location for the 1950s film *Treasure Island*. Gull Rock is now a secure nesting site for guillemots, kittiwakes, herring gulls, cormorants and shags. In winter you may be lucky to spot a great northern diver or a black-throated diver, skimming across the waves amidst gannets, and fulmars.

Walk 25

The Big Beach Walk to Perranporth

A linear walk that leads past some of North Cornwall's best beaches, interspersed by strolls round grassy headlands.

•DISTANCE•	8 miles (12.9km)
•MINIMUM TIME•	4hrs
•ASCENT / GRADIENT•	492ft (150m) ▲▲ ▲▲
•LEVEL OF DIFFICULTY•	🚶 🚶 🚶
•PATHS•	Good coastal footpath and firm sandy beaches, 3 stiles
•LANDSCAPE•	Big sandy beaches and grassy clifftops.
•SUGGESTED MAP•	aqua3 OS Explorer 104 Redruth and St Agnes
•START•	Grid reference: SW 791604 or Grid reference: SW 789608
•FINISH•	Grid reference: SW 756542
•DOG FRIENDLINESS•	Dogs on leads through grazed areas
•PARKING•	Crantock Beach (National Trust), Perranporth Beach car park
•PUBLIC TOILETS•	Crantock village, Crantock Beach car park, Holywell Bay, Perranporth
•NOTE•	Park early at Perranporth and catch the bus to Crantock to the start rather than getting a bus at the end of the walk

Walk 25 Directions

If it's sand you want, this walk offers it in bucketloads. The North Cornish coast from Newquay to Perranporth has some of the finest beaches in Cornwall. Only the brisk bite of the Atlantic and the often massive swells, rob these beaches of true Mediterranean ambience. But, then there's the unbeatable Cornish surf. At Newquay, Holywell Bay and Perranporth, the breakers offer some of the best surfboarding, and bodyboarding in Europe. Just breathing the sparkling air can seem like surfing.

If you start the walk from the National Trust car park above **Crantock Beach**, follow the sandy, enclosed path that leads off a few paces inside the entrance to the car

park, on the left. Follow a footworn grassy path across the dunes of **The Rushy Green**, bearing slightly left towards a half-hidden modern house that has octagonal slate and glass roofs. Near the house, first pass a junction with a path going right, then immediately reach another junction beside two fins of

> **WHILE YOU'RE THERE** ⓘ
> The main attractions of this walk are the various beaches passed en route. If you swim, then you are spoiled for choice. **Crantock Beach** is a delight, all golden sand and sparkling sea. **Porth Joke** is off the beaten beach track, but is fairly small and often damp from the sea and from a stream exit. **Holywell Bay** is another fine beach, though it can become very busy in summer. **Perranporth Beach** is over two miles long and offers everything from reasonable seclusion at its northern end to close-quarters humanity at its more accessible southern end.

Walk 25

grey rock. (If you start from the centre of **Crantock village**, you should head down **Beach Road**, then immediately turn off left along a track. This is **Green Lane**; it leads you to the junction at the two fins of grey rock.)

Facing west, follow the path straight ahead from the fins of rock. In a few paces reach a crossing of sandy tracks. Go straight ahead into an open field, then turn right and follow the field edge and continue round the grassy headland of **Pentire Point West** to reach the narrow inlet of **Porth Joke**, or **Polly Joke**, whose name may derive from the Cornish word *chogha* for 'jackdaw'. Cross the head of the beach and follow the coast path round **Kelsey Head** until you reach the dunes of **Holywell Bay**. Follow a path through the dunes to reach a stream at a broad open area. Here you can divert inland along a sandy track to public toilets and to shops, a café and the inn. (You can regain the coast path and beach by following a path to the left of St Piran's Inn.) Otherwise cross the back of the beach from the broad open area to a stile by a notice that gives advice for passing the **Penhale Army Training Area** ahead.

Follow the coast path steeply uphill. Where it levels off, just past a wooden post, bear up left to pass between a circular compound of metal aerials and a wired-off mine shaft. It is easy to miss this move. (The more obvious path leading downhill ends at the cliff edge, rather spectacularly.) Continue alongside the perimeter of the army camp, paying close attention to footpath signs. The path winds round the seaward face of Ligger Point and soon the long sweep of

---

WHAT TO LOOK FOR ℹ

The sand dunes of this section of Cornish coast support a fascinating range of flowering plants that are specially adapted to survive in the salt laden environment of the sea shore. One of the most distinctive is the sea holly, easily distinguished by its greeny-blue, spiky leaves and pale blue flowers.

Perranporth Beach comes into view. Just beyond a gap and a stile, you reach a junction above the beach itself. Keep left and follow the obvious path until you are above the beach, then descend a sandy slope to the beach. (The lower, right-hand branch of the junction leads to an awkward cliff descent and is not advised.) This part of the beach is a **designated naturist area**, so be prepared to encounter people who are completely naked as you make your way across the the sands.

From here it is a delightful walk along the tideline until you reach the popular and usually crammed southern section of the beach. From here you climb a concrete rampway onto the top of the cliff. Where steps lead up left to a car park, keep straight on up the ramp to a turning area. Join the coast path beyond a crash barrier and stroll on to **Perranporth** itself where the final stretch of sand quite often disappears completely under the massed ranks of sun lovers.

WHERE TO EAT AND DRINK ℹ

Early in the walk the coast path passes the **Crantock Bay Hotel** where you can enjoy morning coffee, lunch or afternoon tea. At Holywell Bay there's a café and the **St Piran's Inn**. In summer there are often small refreshment shacks on Holywell Beach and mid-way along Perranporth Beach. There are pubs and cafés at Crantock and Perranporth.

Walk 26

A Walk Through the Bishop's Wood

A short and gentle stroll through the richly diverse woodlands of a forestry estate near Truro.

•DISTANCE•	3½ miles (5.7km)
•MINIMUM TIME•	2hrs 30min
•ASCENT / GRADIENT•	164ft (50m) ▲ ▲▲
•LEVEL OF DIFFICULTY•	🚶 🚶 🚶
•PATHS•	Forest tracks and paths. Can be very muddy after rain
•LANDSCAPE•	Mixed woodland
•SUGGESTED MAP•	aqua3 OS Explorer 105 Falmouth & Mevagissey
•START / FINISH•	Grid reference: SW 820477
•DOG FRIENDLINESS•	Dogs are welcomed throughout the woods. The authorities ask that owners clear up their dog's mess in the car park and first sections of forest tracks
•PARKING•	Forestry car park, north of Idless, near Truro
•PUBLIC TOILETS•	None on route
•NOTE•	Car park gates are closed at sunset. Working woodland, please take note of notices advising work in progress

BACKGROUND TO THE WALK

Going down to the woods in Cornwall is always a delightful antidote to the county's surfeit of sea. Coastal woodlands do not always offer such an escape; views of the sea, the sound of the sea, and even the smell of the sea keep intruding. At leafy enclaves such as Bishop's Wood near Truro, however, you can safely bury the anchor deep inland. Bishop's Wood is a part of the much larger St Clement Woods that lie a few miles north of Truro and just north of the village of Idless. It acquired its name from the time it was owned by the Bishop of Exeter during the late medieval period. Long before this, probably when the ancient woodland of the area had already been stripped bare by the early farmers, the highest point of the wood was crowned by a fortified Iron Age settlement from which the surrounding countryside could be easily viewed.

Woodland Industry

Today, the substantial banks of the settlement survive, muffled by dense woodland cover. In later centuries, when tree cover was re-established here, the area would have been a typical working woodland. The mix of broad-leaved trees that makes up much of the area indicates long-established forestry. The Iron Age site is densely covered with coppiced oaks. You can identify them by their multiple trunks at the base. When the woods were actively managed for coppicing, the trunks would be cut so that new growth started in several places at once. They would be allowed to grow like this for up to 20 years or so before being harvested for charcoal making, basket making or a host of other wood products. Up to the beginning of the 20th century many woods were managed in this way. The practice is being re-introduced in some areas in Cornwall, because of its beneficial effects on wildlife habitats.

Eerie Track

The walk starts from the forestry car park at the south end of the woods and leads along its eastern edge through Lady's Wood, on a track that is wonderfully eerie and enclosed. A robust little stream runs below the track. Beech trees dominate the cover here and further into the wood, oak, hazel, birch, Japanese larch and holly lie to either side of the track. In spring the trees are bright with fresh leaves; the soft yellow and cream hazel and willow catkins are dusted with pollen and the rich earth beneath the trees supports a wealth of plants, ferns and mosses. Look particularly for wood sorrel, bluebells, three-cornered leeks, and the feathery fronds of male ferns.

The track leads on to the top end of the wood just before Lanner Mill. Here you turn uphill and onto a broad forestry ride that leads back south along the higher ridge of the woods. Halfway along you can divert left from the track to visit the site of the Iron Age settlement. The large bank and ditch that encircled the site is still visible. The rigid upper branches of the numerous coppiced oak trees enclose the central trunks of the trees like cages. This is a well-preserved site although the tree growth and associated scrub blur the full impact of the very large bank and ditch construction. Such hilltop sites date from the transition between the Bronze Age and Iron Age and reflect a growing territorialism amongst early Britons.

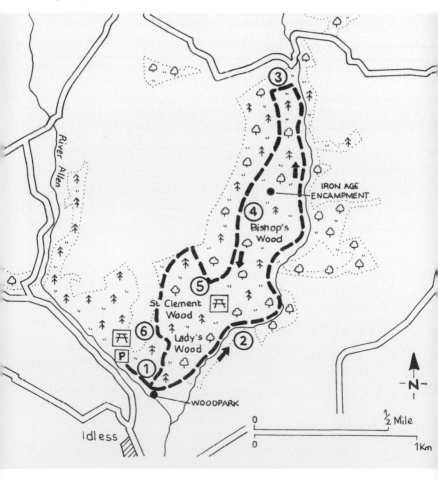

Walk 26

Commercial Centres

These were not forts in the narrow sense of being built purely for defence. They were defensible sites, certainly, but they were commercial and cultural centres as much as anything else, being the focus of a large territory of scattered farmsteads and settlements from which the unforested hilltop site would be easily seen. The hilltop 'fort' or 'castle' represented a central refuge in times of trouble, but served also as a place to bring livestock to market and to exchange household goods and to socialise and celebrate. From the Iron Age site, the last part of the walk takes you onto even higher ground and through newly planted conifers; the young trees are still low enough to afford a distant glimpse of the elegant spires of Truro's cathedral, a fitting view from a Bishop's Wood.

Walk 26 Directions

① Leave the top end of the car park via the wooden barrier and go along a broad track. In a few paces at a fork, keep to the right fork and follow the track above **Woodpark** and along the inside edge of the wood. This track can be very muddy after rain.

② Keep on the main track, parallel to the river, ignoring branch tracks leading off to the left.

③ Just before the northern end of the wood reach a fork. Keep to the main track as it bends left and uphill. The track levels off and at an open area merges with a broad forestry ride. Keep ahead along this ride.

④ At a forestry notice indicating the site of the remains of an I**ron Age encampment**, go left along a

path beneath conifer trees to reach the bank and ditch of the encampment. Return to the main track and turn left.

⑤ At a bend beside a wooden bench, where tracks lead off to left and right, go right and follow a public footpath uphill. At a path crossing turn left and follow the path through scrubland and young pine trees.

> **WHAT TO LOOK FOR** ⓘ
>
> Old woods are often rich in fungi. Look for the trunks of dead trees and you may find the great plate-like layers of various bracket fungi. Other fungi to look for among the rich humus of the woodland underlayer are stinkhorn fungus, the rudely unmistakable *Phallus impudicus*. On oak trees you may find little round wood-like growths known popularly as 'oak apples'. These are produced by gall wasps laying their eggs on oak leaves. The oak apple grows round the egg to protect it during incubation. Look closely and you may see a tiny hole where the adult insect has emerged.

> **WHERE TO EAT AND DRINK** ⓘ
>
> There are no food and drink outlets on the walk and the immediate area is quite isolated; but **Truro** is only a few miles (km) away and there is a pub at **Shortlanesend** about 1 mile (1.6km) to the west of Idless.

⑥ Re-enter mature woodland and follow a track downhill. Keep right at a junction, then go left at the next junction. Reach a T-junction with a broad track. Turn right and follow the track to the **car park**.

A Waterside Walk by the Fal Estuary

From Mylor Churchtown to Flushing in a quiet peninsula world still dominated by ships and sails.

Walk 27

•DISTANCE•	4 miles (6.4km)
•MINIMUM TIME•	3hrs
•ASCENT / GRADIENT•	164ft (50m) ▲ ▲ ▲
•LEVEL OF DIFFICULTY•	🚶 🚶 🚶
•PATHS•	Good paths throughout. Wooded section to Trelew Farm is often very wet, 7 stiles
•LANDSCAPE•	Wooded peninsula flanked by river estuaries and creeks
•SUGGESTED MAP•	aqua3 OS Explorer 105 Falmouth & Mevagissey
•START / FINISH•	Grid reference: SW 820352
•DOG FRIENDLINESS•	Dogs on lead through grazed areas.
•PARKING•	Mylor Churchtown car park
•PUBLIC TOILETS•	Mylor Churchtown and Flushing

BACKGROUND TO THE WALK

The inner estuary of the River Fal, the Carrick Roads, is reputedly the third largest natural harbour in the world. It has welcomed all manner of vessels, from Tudor warships to fishing fleets, to modern cargo vessels and oil rigs and a growing number of yachts. Part of the long maritime heritage of the Fal belongs to the Post Office Packet Service that was responsible for communications throughout the British Empire. The Packet Service was based in the Fal from 1689 to 1850. It was a glorious and freebooting period of British seafaring. Fast Packet vessels ran south to Spain and Portugal and then on to the Americas. The Packet sailors were notorious for their opportunism and many a Packet ship returned from a trip with more than half its cargo as contraband goods. The main Packet base was at Falmouth, but Mylor was a servicing and victualling yard for the Packet boats and many of the Packet captains lived at Flushing in what was effectively maritime suburbia.

Leisure Sailing

At Mylor today, maritime traditions are as strong as ever, as far as leisure sailing goes. Boatyards still bustle with work and local sailing clubs thrive. A gold medal winner in sailing at the 2000 Olympics in Australia, Ben Ainslie, learned many of his skills as a Laser dinghy sailor in these waters and today every creek and inlet of the Fal is dense with sailing and leisure craft. Modern Flushing is an exquisitely peaceful backwater, within shouting distance of bustling Falmouth, but with the river between.

Wooded Valley

The walk takes you from Mylor along the shores of the blunt headland between Mylor Creek and the Penryn River and on to Flushing, in full view of Falmouth docks and waterfront. Flushing is a charming enclave of handsome houses, many with distinctly Dutch features. At Point ④ on the walk, note the plaque opposite, commemorating the Post Office Packet service. From Flushing you turn inland and on to a delightful old track that runs down a wooded valley to the tree-shrouded waters of Mylor Creek from where quiet lanes lead back to St Mylor Church. Here in a churchyard that resonates with maritime history, stands the Ganges Memorial, a commemoration of 53 youngsters who died, mainly of disease, on the famous Royal Naval training ship HMS Ganges that was based at Mylor from 1866 to 1899.

Walk 27 Directions

① From the car park entrance at **Mylor Churchtown**, turn right to the start of a surfaced walkway, signposted to Flushing. Follow the walkway, then, by the gateway of a house, bear left along a path signposted to **Flushing**. Pass in front of **Restronguet Sailing Club**, go up some steps and turn left along the coast path.

② Follow the path round **Penarrow Point** and continue round **Trefusis Point**. Reach a gate and granite grid stile by a wooden shack at **Kilnquay Wood**. Continue to a lane.

> **WHERE TO EAT AND DRINK** ⓘ
> Half-way through the route, at Flushing, there are two good pubs, the **Seven Stars Inn** and the **Royal Standard Inn**. At Mylor Bridge there is a restaurant on the waterfront, the **HMS Ganges Restaurant**.

Walk 27

③ Follow the surfaced lane round left, then go right through a gap beside a gate and continue along a public road. Where the road drops down towards the water's edge, bear right up a surfaced slope to reach the delightful grassy area of the 'Bowling Green'. (Strictly no dog fouling please.) Continue past a little pavilion and toilets and go down a surfaced walkway, then turn left by a junction and signpost into Flushing.

④ Turn right at a street junction and go along Trefusis Road past the Seven Stars Inn. At a junction by the Royal Standard Inn, keep right past the Post Office and go up Kersey Road. At the top of the road, by Orchard Vale, go left up steps, signposted 'Mylor Church'. Cross a stile and keep to the field edge to reach an isolated house and to a stile made of granite bollards.

⑤ In a few paces go right through a gate then turn left over a cattle grid and follow the drive to a public road, Penarrow Road. Cross with care, and go down the road opposite for 30yds (27m), then go right down steps and on down the field edge. Keep straight ahead where the field edge bends left, and enter shady woods.

⑥ Enter the woodland and keep right at a junction to follow a rocky path that is often a mini stream after heavy rainfall. Go through a gate, keep left at a junction then cross a proper stream. Go through a tiny gate and turn right down a farm track to reach a surfaced lane at Trelew.

⑦ Turn right along the lane, passing an old water pump. When you get to a slipway, keep ahead along the unsurfaced Wayfield Road. Continue along between granite posts and on to join the public road into Mylor Churchtown. Cross the road with care (this is a blind corner) and go through the churchyard of St Mylor Church (please note, the path through the churchyard is not a public right of way). Turn right when you reach the waterfront to find the car park.

WHAT TO LOOK FOR i

The wooded sections of the walk are composed mainly of deciduous trees. Unlike conifer woods, these diverse environments support numerous flowering plants amidst their damp, tangled, humus-rich undergrowth. Look for the pink and red flowers of herb robert and campion and the starry white blooms of greater stitchwort. This latter plant was believed to have curative properties in earlier times; it was ground into a paste and applied to boils and sores. Children in Cornwall were once warned not to touch stitchwort at night or they would become 'pixie-led' and lost in the woods.

St Anthony's Guns and Guiding Lights

A walk on the beautiful Roseland Peninsula, visiting an ancient church, a lighthouse, and an old gun battery.

•DISTANCE•	6½ miles (10.4km)
•MINIMUM TIME•	4hrs
•ASCENT / GRADIENT•	230ft (70m) ▲▲▲
•LEVEL OF DIFFICULTY•	林 林 林
•PATHS•	Excellent coastal and creekside footpaths. May be muddy in places during wet weather, 12 stiles
•LANDSCAPE•	Picturesque headland with open coast on one side and sheltered tidal creek and estuary on the other
•SUGGESTED MAP•	aqua3 OS Explorer 105 Falmouth & Mevagissey
•START / FINISH•	Grid reference: SW 848313
•DOG FRIENDLINESS•	Dogs on lead through grazed areas
•PARKING•	National Trust St Anthony Head car park. Can be busy in summer. For main walk there is alternative parking on the route at Porth Farm (Point ③, SW 868329)
•PUBLIC TOILETS•	St Anthony Head car park and Porth Farm car park

BACKGROUND TO THE WALK

Headlands demand attention. They stick their necks out into seaways, guard the entrance to river estuaries, and can spell disaster to careless seagoers. St Anthony Head on the east side of the Falmouth Estuary deserves more attention than most. It lies at the tip of the most southerly promontory of the beautiful Roseland Peninsula and was always of strategic importance. There was a gun battery on St Anthony Head from the early 19th century until 1957, its purpose being to defend the key port of Falmouth. The lighthouse on the Head was built in 1834. One of its main purposes is to warn vessels of the highly dangerous reefs known as the Manacles that lie offshore from Porthoustock below St Keverne (► Walk 35).

As early as 1805, guns were positioned on St Anthony Head to cover the approaches to Falmouth. By the end of the 19th century the headland had been transformed into a formidable gun battery that remained either active or in readiness until after the Second World War. By 1957 Coastal Artillery was discontinued and the St Anthony Battery was stripped of its ordnance. The site came into the care of the National Trust in 1959.

Towan Beach

The route of this walk starts from above the lighthouse and makes a circuit of the narrow peninsula behind St. Anthony Head. The route encompasses the contrasting water worlds of the open sea and the enclosed Percuil River and tidal inlet of Porth Creek. The first part of the walk lies along the breezy east side of the peninsula. The path soon passes above the cliff-fringed Porthbeor Beach. Another ½ mile (800m) takes you to the splendid Towan Beach within its sheltering bay. From the settlement of Porth, above the beach, the route heads inland and follows the opposite side of the peninsula. Leafy paths wind along the wooded shores of Porth Creek and the Percuil River to pass the 19th-century Place House and St Anthony's Church. Beyond the church a more open coast is reached. On the opposite headland stands the village of St Mawes and across the wider estuary lies busy Falmouth. Here you regain the scent and sound of the sea. The path now takes you south along the sea's edge back to St Anthony Head, where you can visit the lighthouse at certain times and divert also to the old Observation Post on the high ground above, (► While You're There).

Walk 28 Directions

① Leave the St Anthony Head car park at its far end and keep straight ahead along a surfaced lane past a row of holiday cottages on the left. Follow the coast path, running parallel with the old military road alongside **Drake's Downs**, to where it passes above **Porthbeor Beach** at a junction with the beach access path, (Walk 29 goes inland here).

② Follow the coast path round **Porthmellin Head** and **Killigerran Head** to reach **Towan Beach**. At the junction with the beach access path, turn left and inland. Bear off left before a gate and go through a roofed passageway, there are toilets on the left, to reach a road.

Walk 28

③ Go straight across the road and through a gapway, signed for 'Porth Farm', then go down a surfaced drive. Turn into the entrance to the National Trust car park, then bear off left along a grassy path signposted 'Place via Percuil River'. Soon cross a footbridge, then turn right. Follow the edge of Froe Creek to a stile into the woods, then follow a path alongside Porth Creek and through Drawler Plantation, ignoring side paths to 'Bohortha'.

④ Pass a small jetty where the St Mawes ferry picks up passengers. Continue to a kissing gate and onto the road end in front of Place House. Go left along the road and uphill.

⑤ Turn right and cross a stile by a red gate, signposted 'Church of St Anthony and St Anthony Head'. Follow the path past the gravestones to the church. Keep dogs under control here. Go up the steps opposite the church door and follow a shady path uphill. Bear right, then, at a T-junction with a track, turn right. Follow the track ahead then, at a bend, bear

> **WHILE YOU'RE THERE** ⓘ
> St Anthony Lighthouse is open to visitors at certain times, depending on lighthouse duties. Halfway up the path between lighthouse and car park, you can divert to the right along a path that takes you to a preserved Battery Observation Post and to a bird hide overlooking the cliffs at Zone Point.

off to the left. Go over a stile by a gate, then follow the edge of the field uphill. Cross over a stile, (there's a seat to your left) and keep straight ahead and downhill until you get to the water's edge.

⑥ Turn left and follow the coast path around Carricknath Point. Just past Great Molunan Beach, cross a causewayed dam above a small quay, then, at a junction, keep right and follow the coast path signs. At a junction with a surfaced track coming down from the left, keep straight ahead to St Anthony Lighthouse.

⑦ Return to the junction and climb the steep, surfaced track to reach the car park. Halfway up, another track leads off right to the preserved Battery Observation Post and to the bird hide above Zone Point,

> **WHAT TO LOOK FOR** ⓘ
> In the sheltered waters of Porth Creek and the Percuil River, look out for the heron and other wading birds such as curlews and oyster catchers. The latter is unmistakable because of its glossy black breast and back feathers, its snow-white underparts and its distinctive orange bill. Around St Anthony Head, the various viewpoints, such as the Battery Observation Post and the bird hide at Zone Point, offer opportunities for spotting seabirds such as the fulmar, cormorant, kittiwake, and gannet. The gannet's beak is made of bone and the bird's skull is exceptionally strong to help cushion the explosive impact it makes when diving at speed into the sea in pursuit of fish. However, gannets eventually develop poor eyesight because of repeated impact with the water and sadly many die from diving onto underground reefs that they mistake for shoals of fish.

The Church of St Anthony and St Anthony Head

A closer look at the furthest reaches of Roseland Peninsula.
See map and information panel for Walk 28

•DISTANCE•	4 miles (6.4km)
•MINIMUM TIME•	2hrs 30min
•ASCENT / GRADIENT•	230ft (70m) ▲▲▲
•LEVEL OF DIFFICULTY•	🚶🚶🚶

Walk 29 Directions (Walk 28 option)

This shorter version of the Walk 28 concentrates on the most westerly end of the Roseland Peninsula around **St Anthony Head**. You follow the main walk as far as the cliff above **Porthbeor Beach**. Here, turn inland along the access path to the beach to reach the road that runs down the spine of the peninsula.

Turn right along the road, then, in just a few paces go left, signposted '**Bohortha**'. Follow the lane through the quiet hamlet and where the surfaced road ends, take the track ahead, signposted '**Place Quay and Church of St Anthony**'. In turn this track ends at a three-way signpost, Point Ⓐ.

Go over the stile, signposted '**Church of St Anthony**', then follow the field edge downhill to reach a narrow stile on the right, and a steep flight of descending steps that takes you to a surfaced lane. Cross the road diagonally right to the stile by the red gate (Point ⑤ on main route).

From here the directions are the same as on the main walk. The path to St Anthony Church runs amidst randomly sited gravestones that lie beneath overarching trees, a serene little cemetery. The church is a remarkable building, screened by its surrounding trees and by the rather clumsy 19th-century neo-Gothic, **Place House**. The church is now in the care of the Churches Conservation Trust.

St Anthony was once part of a 12th-century priory and its intrinsic 13th-century identity survived the wholesale rebuilding of most Cornish churches that took place in the 15th century. It also survived a Victorian restoration and is a compelling example of an early medieval Cornish church. The exquisite south doorway is a fine piece of Romanesque design and has a nicely eccentric accent in the form of an off-centre medallion in the arch. Inside the church, the central crossing is a wonderful 13th-century survival.

> **WHERE TO EAT AND DRINK** ℹ️
> There are no refreshment opportunities anywhere along the route. In summer there is often an ice cream and soft drinks van at **St Anthony Head** car park.

A Long Walk Through Historic Falmouth

A town walk through the busy port reveals a fascinating slice of Cornwall's maritime history.

•DISTANCE•	3 miles (4.8km)
•MINIMUM TIME•	4hrs
•ASCENT / GRADIENT•	197ft (60m) ▲▲▲
•LEVEL OF DIFFICULTY•	🚶 🚶 🚶
•PATHS•	Surfaced walkways and paths throughout. Very steep steps descent at end of walk
•LANDSCAPE•	Townscape and seafront
•SUGGESTED MAP•	Falmouth Town Map
•START / FINISH•	Grid reference: SW 805327
•DOG FRIENDLINESS•	Dog fouling of streets is prohibited
•PARKING•	Quarry Car Park, Quarry Hill. Hornworks Car Park, Pendennis Castle
•PUBLIC TOILETS•	Webber Street, Prince of Wales Quay, North Quay Arwenack Street, Cliff Road

Walk 30 Directions

Modern Falmouth still belongs to the waterfront that created it. A succession of quays protrudes, at intervals, along nearly 1½ miles (2.4km) of waterfront and, in the shelter of **Pendennis Point**, lie substantial dockyards. On the crown of the Point, **Pendennis Castle** survives as one of the finest examples of Tudor fortifications in Britain. On Falmouth's southern shore lie palatial hotels, ornamental gardens and parades. Everything about Falmouth reflects the sea and seagoing and this walk takes in most facets of that great maritime heritage.

The walk starts from **the Moor**, once a tidal creek and now a rather traffic-bound focal point of the town's busy commercial life. Walk down **Killigrew Street** on the south side of the Moor, then cross **High Street** onto the **Prince of Wales Quay** from where you get a long view of Falmouth's waterfront. Return from the Quay and turn left into **Market Street**, the first of Falmouth's linked main thoroughfares. Market Street merges with **Church Street**, which in turn merges with **Arwenack Street** at the handsome **Church of St Charles the Martyr**. All the way along these busy, shop-lined streets you can divert left to the waterfront quays of **Fish House Quay** by the **Grapes Inn**, **Upton Slip** in Church Street, where you find the colourful figurehead of an old ship, the *Amazon*, and **Custom House Quay**, reached from **Arwenack Street**. Here you find a tall red-brick chimney stack, the **King's Pipe**, once used to burn smuggled tobacco confiscated by excisemen.

Walk 30

From the end of **Arwenack Street** continue along **Grove Place** and **Bar Road**, passing the well-preserved medieval manor **house of Arwenack** on the right. Opposite Arwenack is an ugly granite obelisk of the late 18th century. Cross over at a junction with **Avenue Road**, then, opposite the entrance to **Falmouth Docks**, bear right and go under a railway bridge. Cross, with care, at a roundabout, then continue up the road opposite, signposted '**Pendennis Castle**' (► While You're There for route to castle). Keep right at the top of the rise and go along **Castle Drive**, then turn right into **Cliff Road**.

Pass above the south-facing **Castle Beach** and **Tunnel Beach**, into 'seaside resort' Falmouth. On the inland side of the road stands a line of handsome hotels. Reach an eerie well-staircase that leads down to a tunnel and a viewpoint. At road level ahead is a little Gothic folly. Cross **Cliff Road**, just before the

folly, and with care, and go up the left hand walkway of **Gyllyngdune Gardens**. Go down right, where the walkway forks, and pass through a little sunken garden, then continue up the other side past two shell grottoes, to reach a gate into the marvellous garden patio of the **Princess Pavilion**. Leave by the opposite corner and pass by the theatre box office, going left, then right, then left again and out of the Pavilion gates. Turn down right to a T-junction with **Melvill Road**. Cross the road diagonally right and go down some steps, then turn right along **Avenue Road**.

Follow the road downhill and go beneath a railway bridge, then turn left along the central, tree-lined parade of **Arwenack Avenue**. Walk between the flanking pillars at the end of the avenue, cross the street and keep ahead along **Gyllyng Street** to its end. Keep up to the left by a telephone kiosk and then continue along **Vernon Place**. Bear round to the left by the **Jacob's Ladder** pub, then, just opposite the pub, turn right, brace yourself, and descend carefully back to **the Moor** down **Jacob's Ladder**. The 111 steps were built here by a local merchant, Jacob Hamblyn, in the 19th century as a more convenient link between his house and workshop.

High Cliffs and a High Hill at St Agnes

A bracing walk along the cliffs at St Agnes, followed by an inland climb to the top of St Agnes Beacon.

•DISTANCE•	5 miles (8km)
•MINIMUM TIME•	3hrs
•ASCENT / GRADIENT•	623ft (190m) ▲▲▲
•LEVEL OF DIFFICULTY•	🚶 🚶 🚶
•PATHS•	Good coastal footpaths and inland tracks
•LANDSCAPE•	Dramatic coastal cliffs and a high heath-covered hill
•SUGGESTED MAP•	aqua3 OS Explorer 104 Redruth & St Agnes
•START / FINISH•	Grid reference: SW 699512
•DOG FRIENDLINESS•	Dogs on lead through grazed areas
•PARKING•	St Agnes Head. Number of parking spaces along the clifftop track. Start the walk from any of these
•PUBLIC TOILETS•	Chapel Porth Beach

BACKGROUND TO THE WALK

The awesome sea cliffs of St Agnes Head are well hidden from above. There is no easy view, unless you are a very skilled rock climber. On St Agnes Head and on Carn Gowla, the cliff that runs south from the headland, vast 300ft (90m) high walls of rock soar from an ever restless sea. They do not end at clear-cut edges, however. Instead they merge with gentle slopes of grass and heather that in turn rise gently to the cliff top. Yet you are always aware of the exhilarating exposure of these great gulfs as you stroll safely by.

Promontory

This walk takes you along the flat cliff top tracks and past the little promontory of Tubby's Head, once an Iron Age settlement fortified by an earth embankment across its neck. From here you pass through what was once an industrious mining landscape that is signposted by the remains of mine buildings such as the mighty Towanroath Shaft, a granite castle-keep of a building standing directly above the sea amidst swathes of pink thrift and cream-coloured bladder campion in summer. Built in 1872, this was the pumping house for the Wheal Coates mine whose buildings, further uphill, you see from the coast path. Flooding of the deeper Cornish mines was always a major problem and separate pumping houses were built to draw up water and eject it through tunnels, known as adits, in the cliff face below. The buildings of Towanroath Shaft were skilfully restored by the National Trust in the early 1970s.

Chapel Porth

Beyond Towanroath the path descends into Chapel Porth where you can enjoy the delights of a typical Cornish beach; but during the 19th century the entire valley floor that leads down to the cove was given over to the processing of the mineral ore that came from dozens of tin and copper mines, scattered across the surrounding landscape. As you walk up the valley, you pick your way through a landscape now overgrown by nature, but that was once subdued by industry. From the valley floor the route leads up a delightful valley, protected from the harsh onshore weather by high ground. Soon, you climb onto the bare, rounded summit of St Agnes Beacon, 629ft (192m) high and a superb viewpoint. As the name makes clear, this prominent hilltop was used traditionally for the lighting of signal fires and for celebratory bonfires. From the Beacon's airy heights you drop down effortlessly to the coast once more.

Walk 31 Directions

① Join the coastal footpath from wherever you park along the cliff top. Follow the stony track across **Tubby's Head**. Branch off right onto a narrower path about 100yds (91m) before old mine buildings (these are the remains of **Wheal Coates mine**). Cross a stone stile

and continue to **Towanroath mine engine house**.

② About 50yds (46m) beyond Towanroath branch off right at a signpost and descend to **Chapel Porth Beach**.

③ Cross the stream at the back corner of the car park and follow a path up **Chapel Combe** next to the

WHERE TO EAT AND DRINK ⓘ
There is a seasonal café at **Chapel Porth**, at the midway point of the walk. **St Agnes** village has a couple of good pubs where you can get bar meals.

WHAT TO LOOK FOR ⓘ
In summer the heathery vegetation of the St Agnes cliff tops and the inland hill of the Beacon attract a wealth of butterflies such as the grayling, a brown-coloured butterfly distinguished by the black edges to its wings and the two white-pupilled spots on its fore wings. It feeds on wild thyme and heather and often perches on the rocks. Another butterfly to look out for here is the green hairstreak. It is golden-brown on its upper wings and distinctively green on its under side.

stream. Pass below a mine building and where the path forks among trees, go left through a wooden kissing gate.

④ Cross a bridge then turn right onto a track. Continue along a grassy track. Where the track narrows, keep ahead at a fork. Keep alongside a field and onto a track, turn left over a wooden stile by a gate onto a track. After 50yds (46m), reach a junction with a wide track. Turn left and continue to a public road.

WHILE YOU'RE THERE ⓘ
Spend some time in **St Agnes**, a highly individual village with some fascinating features including a picturesque stepped terrace of houses known famously as **Stippy Stappy**, one of the most photographed subjects in Cornwall. St Agnes's beach is at **Trevaunance Cove**, to the north of the village.

⑤ Turn right along the public road, and keep ahead at a junction. In 200yds (183m), next to the entrance to the **Sunholme Hotel**, continue up a stony track on the left. After 50yds (46m), at a junction, go left and follow a path rising to the obvious summit of **St Agnes Beacon**.

⑥ From the summit of the Beacon follow the lower of two tracks, heading north west, down towards a road. Just before you reach the road turn right along a narrow path, skirting the base of the hill, eventually emerging at the road by a seat.

⑦ Cross over and follow the track opposite, across **New Downs**, directly to the edge of the cliffs, then turn left at a junction with the coast path and return to the **car park**.

Mines and Methodism at Redruth

A walk through Cornwall's mining heartland, visiting Methodism's famous outdoor 'cathedral' of Gwennap Pit along the way.

•DISTANCE•	4 miles (6.4km)
•MINIMUM TIME•	2hrs 30min
•ASCENT / GRADIENT•	442ft (135m)
•LEVEL OF DIFFICULTY•	
•PATHS•	Field paths, rough tracks and surfaced lanes. Can be muddy after rain, 6 stiles
•LANDSCAPE•	Small fields and open heathland with quarry and mine remains
•SUGGESTED MAP•	aqua3 OS Explorer 104 Redruth & St Agnes
•START / FINISH•	Grid reference: SW 699421
•DOG FRIENDLINESS•	Dogs on lead through grazed areas
•PARKING•	Several car parks in Redruth
•PUBLIC TOILETS•	Redruth car parks. Gwennap Pit Visitor Centre, when open

BACKGROUND TO THE WALK

The old Cornish town of Redruth gained its name from mineral mining. In medieval times, the process of separating tin and copper from waste materials turned a local river blood-red with washed out iron oxide. The Cornish name for a nearby ford was Rhyd Druth, the 'ford of the red' and the village that grew around it became Redruth. The innovative engineering that developed in tandem with mining, turned Redruth and its adjoining town of Camborne into centres of Cornish industry.

Religious Zeal

Into the often bleak world of 18th-century mineral mining came the brothers John and Charles Wesley, their religious zeal as hot as a Redruth furnace. It's very appropriate that one of the most revered locations in Methodism is Gwennap Pit, near Redruth. Here the grassy hollow of a caved-in mine shaft was first used for secular gatherings and events, which included cock-fighting. But it wasn't long before the pit was commandeered as a sheltered venue for preaching. John Wesley preached here on 18 occasions between 1762 and 1789 and, in 1806, Gwennap Pit was transformed into the neat hollow of concentric turfed seating that you see today. Despite this 200 year legacy its freehold was not secured by the Methodist Church until 1978.

High Ground

The first part of this walk leads from the heart of Redruth past such significant mining relics as the great chimney stack of the Pednandrea Mine, just off Sea View Terrace. Once the stack towered eight storeys high; it's now reduced to four, but is still impressive. From here you soon climb to the high ground of Gwennap and Carn Marth. The field path that takes you to Gwennap Pit was once a 'highway' of people heading for this 'Cathedral of the moor'.

Today there is a Visitor Centre at the Pit, alongside the peaceful little Busveal Chapel of 1836.

From Gwennap Pit the walk leads onto the summit of Carn Marth and to one of the finest viewpoints in Cornwall; unexpectedly so because of the hill's modest profile. From above the flooded quarry on the summit you look north to the sea and to the hill of St Agnes Beacon (▶ Walk 31). North east lies the St Austell clay country, south west is the rocky summit of Carn Brea with its distinctive granite cross; south east you can even see the cranes on Falmouth dockside. From the top of Carn Marth, the return route is all downhill along rough tracks and quiet country lanes that lead back to the heart of Redruth.

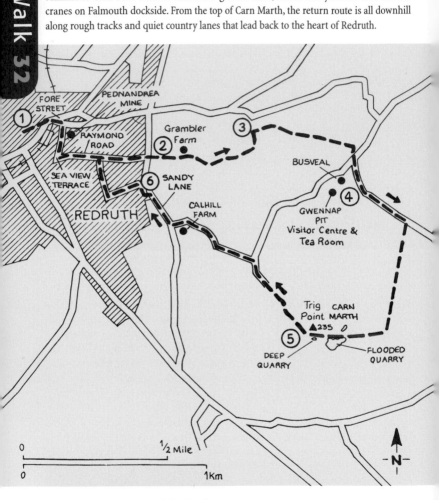

Walk 32 Directions

① From any of the car parks, make your way to **Fore Street**, the main street of Redruth. Walk up to a three-way junction (the railway station is down to the right) and take the middle branch, to the left of **Redruth Methodist Church**,

signposted 'To Victoria Park'. This is **Wesley Street**. In just a few paces turn right on **Sea View Terrace**; the chimney stack of the **Pednandrea Mine** (▶ While You're There) is up to the left a few paces along the road. Pass **Basset Street** on the right and, where the streets cross, go left up **Raymond Road** to a T-junction with **Sandy Lane**.

② Cross the road with care, then follow the track opposite, signposted '**Public Bridleway**' and '**Grambler Farm**'. Go through a gate by the farm and continue to an open area. Bear left here and follow a much narrower track between hedges. When you reach a junction with another track turn left, signposted '**Gwennap Pit**'.

③ Go right, following the signposts for **Gwennap Pit**, and cross a stile by a gate, then go through a small wooden gate. Keep ahead (there may be free-ranging pigs in the area so dogs should be kept under strict control). Go over a stile at the next gate and then follow the edge of the field ahead. Cross a final field towards a house and then walk down a lane past the house to a junction of surfaced roads at **Busveal**. Cross over and follow the road opposite for 100yds (91m) to **Gwennap Pit**.

WHERE TO EAT AND DRINK ⓘ

There is a small tea room at the Gwennap Pit Visitor Centre, which is open May–September, Monday–Friday 10–12:30 and 2–4:30; Saturday 10–12:30. You can picnic in Gwennap Pit itself, but please don't leave any litter. Redruth has several pleasant restaurants, cafés and pubs to choose from. Sample the wonderful local Cornish pasties from WC Rowe's in Fore Street. The **Red Lion** pub is also in Fore Street, and there is a fish and chip shop in Green Lane.

---

④ Follow the road away from **Gwennap Pit**. In about 300yds (274m) turn off to the right along a broad track, signposted '**Public Bridleway**'. Keep ahead at two crossings, then, at a final crossing beside a ruined building, turn right and follow a stony track up the hill to the prominent summit of **Carn Marth**.

WHAT TO LOOK FOR ⓘ

The field hedgerows throughout the walk are bright with wild flowers in spring and summer. Butterflies brighten the scene even more. Look for the handsome peacock butterfly (*Nymphalidae*), that feeds on the nectar of bramble flowers and also on the juice of berries. The brownish-red peacock is easily identified by the 'peacock-eye' markings on its hind wings.

---

⑤ Pass a flooded quarry (there's a viewpoint on the far side), then just beyond a trig point, bear round right on a path alongside the fenced-in rim of a deep quarry. On reaching a surfaced lane, turn left. Turn left at the next junction. Follow the lane to a T-junction with a road at **Calhill Farm**. Turn right and walk along **Sandy Road**, keeping a careful watch for traffic, for 275yds (251m).

⑥ Go left at a junction, signposted as a cycle route, and follow a lane round right, then left into a broad avenue of houses. At a crossroads turn right along **Trefusis Road**. At the next junction turn left into **Raymond Road** and then turn right into **Sea View Terrace**. Turn left down **Wesley Street** and on into **Fore Street**.

WHILE YOU'RE THERE ⓘ

A visit to **Gwennap Pit** and its visitor centre is irresistible, but Redruth itself rewards exploration. Many buildings in Fore Street are Victorian Gothic and have some unusual features such as decorative brickwork. These, and the Italianate **Clock Tower** of 1828, reflect the boom period of Redruth's growth. The **Pednandrea Mine Chimney Stack**, passed early in the walk, was part of a mine that operated from about 1710 to 1891 producing copper, tin, lead and arsenic. The original height of the stack was between 126 and 140ft (38–43m).

Hidden Creeks of Helford

A circuit of some of the peaceful tidal creeks of the Helford Estuary.

•DISTANCE•	5 miles (8km)
•MINIMUM TIME•	3hrs
•ASCENT / GRADIENT•	328ft (100m) ▲▲ ▲
•LEVEL OF DIFFICULTY•	👫 👫 👫
•PATHS•	Good woodland paths and tracks and field paths. Short section of quiet lane, 10 stiles
•LANDSCAPE•	Wooded creekside and fields
•SUGGESTED MAP•	aqua3 OS Explorer 103 The Lizard
•START / FINISH•	Grid reference: SW 759261
•DOG FRIENDLINESS•	Dogs must be kept under strict control between Treath and St Anthony
•PARKING•	Helford car park. Large car park overlooking creek. Can become busy in summer. Only authorised cars are allowed beyond the car park into the village of Helford
•PUBLIC TOILETS•	Helford car park

BACKGROUND TO THE WALK

The Helford River is enduringly popular with land-based visitors and leisure sailors alike, yet the area manages somehow to absorb it all. Cars probe tentatively between the unforgiving stone hedges of narrow Cornish lanes. The bulk of river craft are yachts, so that on a busy sailing day you will hear only the pleasing flap of sails blowing through, as flocks of vessels tack across the estuary mouth. The pelt of trees that lines the estuary and its subsidiary creeks plays a great part in this muffling of too much human racket.

Picturesque

Yet the picturesque, leisure-dominated Helford of today was once a bustling haven for all sorts of trade, and not least, was a haven for pirates and smugglers. During Elizabethan times especially, a passel of Cornish rascals, from the highest in the land to the lowest, was engaged in plundering the cargoes of vessels that sailed through the Channel approaches. The Helford, as it is popularly known, was a secretive, useful base from which all manner of goods could be spirited away inland. In later times the river became an equally secretive base for missions against German-occupied France during the Second World War.

There is little physical evidence of any of this busy past, but in the shrouded creeks that run off like fibrous roots from the main river it is easy to imagine the utter remoteness of life hundreds of years ago, when movement by sea was far more convenient than by land. This walk starts from the village of Helford and follows the southern shore of the estuary between Treath and Dennis Head, mainly through the deep woodland of the Bosahan estate. There are tantalising glimpses of the river through the trees and the path skirts tiny coves such as Bosahan and Ponsence with their inviting beaches that must surely have seen their share of night-landings in the piratical past.

The return leg of the walk follows the north shore of the adjacent Gillan Creek, far smaller and thus far less accommodating to vessels than the deep Helford. Here the tiny

Church of St Anthony adds to the overall serenity. From near the head of the creek, you climb inland to Manaccan, a charming hamlet that seems to tumble down the slopes of the valley. Beyond the village the route leads into the wooded valley above Helford and takes you back to your starting point through chequered shade.

Walk 33 Directions

① As you leave the car park, turn left along a path, signed '**Coast Path**'. Go through a metal gate and follow a sunken track. Descend steps, then turn right along a lane. At a steep right-hand bend, bear off ahead along a track. Follow this permissive path through trees, keeping left at any junctions.

② Leave the wooded area via a metal gate, then turn left along a field edge to a stone stile, Follow the bottom edge of the next two fields. Cross a fence at a field gap beside a white pole and a red post and triangle (these are navigation marks). Follow the field edge ahead. Go through a kissing gate, then follow the field edge (there's a seat and viewpoint on the left), to where it ends at the beginning of a wide track (to make the short circuit of **Dennis Head**, follow the track ahead to a stile on the left).

③ To continue on the main route, turn sharply right at the start of the wide track and follow the left-hand field edge and then a path across the open field. Join a track behind a house, then go through a kissing gate and descend to **St Anthony's Church**. Follow the road alongside **Gillan Creek**.

④ Just past where the road curves round a bay, go up right between granite gate posts by a public footpath sign. Follow a broad track through trees to houses at

Roscadden. Keep ahead along a track that leads to **Manaccan** at a T-junction opposite **Manaccan Church**.

⑤ Go through the churchyard and on through the gate opposite to a road (the village shop is to the left). Keep ahead to a junction, the New Inn is down to the left, then go up right, past the school. Keep uphill, then turn left along **Minster Meadow**, go over a stile, and through two fields to reach a road.

⑥ Go diagonally left to the stile opposite, cross a field, then go left following signposts to reach woods. Follow the path ahead. At a junction keep ahead, go over a stile and reach a second junction. The extended walk starts here.

⑦ Bear down right and follow a broad track through trees to reach some buildings at **Helford**. Keep ahead on reaching a surfaced road and follow the road uphill to the **car park**.

WHILE YOU'RE THERE ⓘ

There are two churches on the route of the walk, **St Anthony-in-Meneage** and **St Manacca** at Manaccan. Both have some fine features. At St Anthony the piers of the single aisle lean engagingly to port; the 15th-century font has fine reliefs of angels holding shields. Look for the granite drinking bowl, complete with engaging inscription, outside the main door. Manaccan's church has a splendid Norman south door. The church also has a single arcade, but its wagon roofs are well-renovated. There is an ancient fig tree growing out of the wall.

Helford River and Frenchman's Creek

Continue around to the romantically named inlet on the Helston River.
See map and information panel for Walk 33

•DISTANCE•	6½ miles (10.4km)
•MINIMUM TIME•	4hrs
•ASCENT / GRADIENT•	164ft (50m)
•LEVEL OF DIFFICULTY•	

Walk 34 Directions (Walk 33 option)

At the green heart of the **Helford River** lies the impossibly romantic **Frenchman's Creek**. More properly known as **Frenchman's Pill**, this thin finger of tidal water has become famous through its association with the romantic novel *Frenchman's Creek*, by Daphne du Maurier; but the writer Arthur Quiller Couch had written a short story with the same title long before du Maurier's novel appeared and the source of the name is not certain. It was recorded on 19th-century maps and may yet prove to be a corruption of an old usage, or simply a longstanding reference to French ships that must, at one time, have visited the Helford quite regularly.

This extension to the main walk maintains the theme of woods and water. It begins at Point ⑥, where, instead of bearing down right at the junction, you keep straight on through the trees to reach a field. Turn right along the field edge to a gate and then follow the right edge of the next field to another gate onto a track and then on past **Kestle farmhouse** to a surfaced road. Cross the road, then cross a field to a track that leads down to join a public footpath signposted '**Footpath along Frenchman's Creek**' at Point Ⓐ.

The creek is shrouded by trees, but get your tide and timing right and the water gleams through the tangled branches and flickering leaves. The path leads down the east bank of the creek then climbs to a field. Go right where the track forks, signposted '**Helford via Penarvon Cove**'. Just beyond a gate and a cattle grid, turn left down a lane, then fork right to reach **Penarvon Cove.** From the top end of the beach follow a path that leads to a concrete track, where a left turn takes you down past the **Shipwright's Arms** and on through **Helford** village to join the final part of the main walk at Point Ⓑ.

> **WHERE TO EAT AND DRINK** ⓘ
> Ice creams and soft drinks can be bought at **St Anthony** from the sailing shop on the beach. The attractive **New Inn** at Manaccan does pub lunches. The **Shipwright's Inn** at Helford is reached by walking through the village from the car park and serves a range of food.

Walk 35

Rocks and Reefs at St Keverne

A walk of startling contrasts through a coastal and industrial landscape south of the Helford River.

•DISTANCE•	4 miles (6.4km)
•MINIMUM TIME•	3hrs
•ASCENT / GRADIENT•	606ft (185m) ▲▲▲
•LEVEL OF DIFFICULTY•	👫 👫 👫
•PATHS•	Field edge paths, coastal footpath, steeply stepped path, country lanes, 8 stiles
•LANDSCAPE•	Fields, woods and coast
•SUGGESTED MAP•	aqua3 OS Explorer 103 The Lizard
•START / FINISH•	Grid reference: SW 807218
•DOG FRIENDLINESS•	Dogs on lead through grazed areas. Notices indicate
•PARKING•	Large area of parking on grass and gravel above beach. Donation box
•PUBLIC TOILETS•	Porthoustock and St Keverne
•NOTE•	Dean Quarries are working quarries. Please heed all warning notices. Blasting may take place at certain times, usually late afternoon. A custodian is on duty at the coast path approach to the quarry. Please respect his instructions

Walk 35 Directions

The heart has been torn out of the Cornish coast at the great quarries of Porthoustock and Dean Point below the handsome village of St Keverne. There has been an honourable trade in quarrying here for many years and though Porthoustock Quarry no longer operates, Dean Quarries still do. The route of this walk traces its way round the seaward perimeter of Dean Quarries through a desolate yet fascinating industrial landscape.

The walk starts at **Porthoustock Beach**, a vast apron of grey sand and shingle that has been artificially extended by quarry waste. You turn left outside the car park and follow the road steeply uphill, then turn left at the first junction. In another steep 55yds (50m), go right and over a stile, then bear left across three fields to reach a lane. Turning right along this lane takes you to the peaceful little hamlet of **Rosenithon**, where you turn left down a lane by a post box. Where the lane ends, cross a stile by a gate,

---

WHERE TO EAT AND DRINK ⓘ

The walk passes conveniently close to a truly Cornish institution, **Roskilly's**, the working dairy farm of Tregellast Barton, where the Roskilly family have established a famous ice cream parlour and restaurant, and a shop selling mouth watering fudge, jams, chutneys, apple juice and cider. There are two pubs in St Keverne, the **Three Tuns** and the **White Hart Inn**, both of which do bar meals.

WHILE YOU'RE THERE

While you're in St Keverne, visit the **Church of St Akeveranus**. The church's octagonal, ribbed spire was painted white at one time because it could be seen from the sea and was a useful landmark that helped ship's masters avoid the treacherous Manacles reef. The Manacles claimed many vessels, however, and the churchyard has its share of gravestones that commemorate those who drowned.

Walk 35

then bear round left past a house and barn to a stile, (dogs should be kept on lead from here). Go down an enclosed path, and then straight down fields from where there are panoramic views of the infamous wrecking reef of **The Manacles**, ½ mile (800m) offshore.

Once on **Godrevy Beach,** head for the south end to a path beside a quarry warning notice. If blasting is imminent, (usually in the late afternoon, if at all), you will be stopped by a quarry employee until blasting is completed. Continue up the path and then, beyond two huge boulders, bear left down a quarry track to follow footpath notices round the edge of **Dean Point** and its quarried amphitheatres. The path runs alongside dirt tracks and wriggles between heaped banks of shale; it even passes beneath a conveyor belt that carries roadstone to a loading jetty. Finally the path descends to another quarry warning sign. Go right just before the sign and follow a steep path uphill and

continue to a broad gravel track by houses, then turn right to reach a surfaced lane. Turn left here and in just under ½ mile (800m) look for a stile on the right, just before a sharp bend. Use this stile to cut across a field and back onto the lane. At the next, immediate, road junction you can divert left to a farm that is famous for the delicious ice cream it produces. On the main route keep ahead at the junction for ½ mile (800m) to reach **St Keverne** and its landmark church.

Go into the churchyard and follow a footpath to the left of the church. At the bottom corner of the churchyard go through a gate, cross a gravel path, then go through a wooden kissing gate. Follow the edges of fields ahead. Cross a lane and then a stile, then keep to the left edge of a field. Where the field edge bends left, keep ahead following the contour of the field to reach a wooden stile. Cross a small stream, then follow a sunken path into some woods. You are now in a completely different world to the open coast and quarry country, but not for long. Cross a bridge and a stile, follow the stream to reach a right turn, signposted '**Porthoustock**'. At a road, turn left uphill, then in 50yds (46m), turn off right. Cross a stream and a stile, then follow a path beneath trees to reach a lane by thatched cottages from where you descend to **Porthoustock**.

WHAT TO LOOK FOR

At Godrevy Beach, just north of Dean Quarries, a variety of salt-resistant plants covers the inner section of the beach, including sea plantain with its tall greenish spikes, the green-flowered sea beet, sea splurge, and sea bindweed, with its white bell-like flowers. All of these maritime plants are specially equipped to cope with the extremes of their environment, such as seasonal dryness and the punishing effect of salt-laden sea winds. Most have fleshy leaves that absorb and store water and that act as reservoirs against the desiccating effect of salt. They also have long roots that probe deeply for moisture.

The Serpentine Route to Cadgwith

A wandering route between coast and countryside through the serpentine rock landscape of the Lizard Peninsula.

•DISTANCE•	4½ miles (7.2km)
•MINIMUM TIME•	3hrs
•ASCENT / GRADIENT•	230ft (70m)
•LEVEL OF DIFFICULTY•	
•PATHS•	Very good. Occasionally rocky in places. Rock can be slippery when wet.
•LANDSCAPE•	Landlocked lanes and woodland tracks, coastal footpaths high above the sea
•SUGGESTED MAP•	aqua3 OS Explorer 103 The Lizard
•START / FINISH•	Grid reference: SW 720146
•DOG FRIENDLINESS•	Can let dogs off lead on coastal paths, but please keep under strict control on field paths
•PARKING•	Cadgwith car park. About 350yds (320m) from Cadgwith. Busy in summer
•PUBLIC TOILET•	Ruan Minor and Cadgwith

BACKGROUND TO THE WALK

The serpentine rock of the Lizard Peninsula is fascinating by name and by nature. Its geological label, serpentinite, is a word that fails to slither quite so easily off the tongue as does its popular usage 'serpentine'. The name derives from the sinuous veins of green, red, yellow and white that wriggle across the dark green or brownish red surface of the rock. The best serpentine is easily carved and shaped and can be polished to a beautiful sheen. In the 19th century serpentine furnishings were the height of fashion and the material was used for shop fronts and fireplaces. The industry declined during the 1890's however, due to the vagaries of fashion but also because the colourful, curdled stone of The Lizard decayed quickly in polluted urban atmospheres. Serpentine became less popular for use in shop fronts and monuments as cheaper, more resilient marble from Italy and Spain began to dominate the market. Today serpentine craftsmen still operate in little workshops on the Lizard and you can buy serpentine souvenirs at Lizard Village. Throughout this walk there are stiles built of serpentine; their surfaces are mirror-smooth and slippery from use. Admire, but take care when they are wet.

The walk first takes a fittingly wandering route inland to the sleepy village of Ruan Minor from where a narrow lane leads down to the Poltesco Valley. At the mouth of the valley is Carleon Cove, once the site of water wheels, steam engines, machine shops, storehouses and a factory where serpentine was processed. Only a few ruins remain. A narrow harbour pool, almost stagnant now, is dammed on the seaward side by a deep shingle bank where once there was an outlet to the sea. From here, during the heyday of Carleon's serpentine industry, barges loaded with finished pieces were towed out during spells of fine weather to cargo ships awaiting offshore.

Walk 36

Thatched Cottages

From Carleon Cove the coast path is followed pleasantly to Cadgwith, an archetypal Cornish fishing village. Cadgwith has a number of thatched cottages, a rare sight in windy Cornwall, although coverings of wire-mesh on most of them indicate wise precaution against storm damage. Cadgwith still supports a fleet of small fishing boats and is given an enduring identity because of it. Beyond the village the coast path leads to the Devil's Frying Pan, a vast gulf in the cliffs caused by the collapse of a section of coast that had been undermined by the sea. From here the path leads on for a short distance along the edge of the cliffs before the route turns inland to the Church of the Holy Cross at Grade. Two fields beyond the church you find the ancient St Ruan's Well and the road that leads back to the start of this delightfully serpentine ramble.

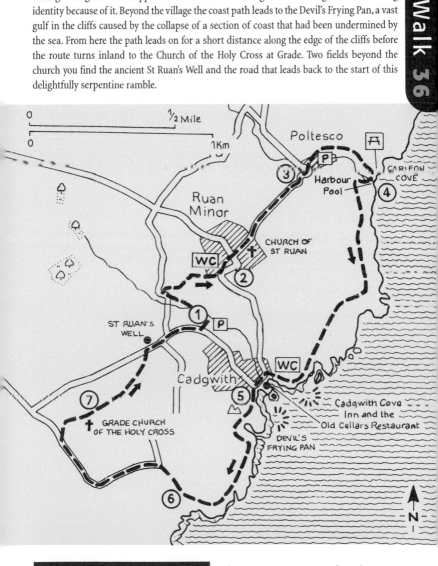

Walk 36 Directions

① Go left along a grassy ride below the car park, to a stile. Continue over another stile, then branch right. Turn right at a lane, then on the corner, go up a track and continue to the main road at **Ruan Minor**.

② Go left and, just beyond the shop, turn left down a surfaced path. Rejoin the main road by a thatched cottage (there are toilets just before the road). Cross diagonally right, then go down a lane past the **Church of St Ruan**.

③ Just past an old mill and a bridge, go right at a T-junction to reach the car park at **Poltesco**. From the far end of the car park follow a track, signposted '**Carleon Cove**'. Go right at a junction.

> **WHAT TO LOOK FOR** ⓘ
>
> Water is often slow to drain on the soil of the Cadgwith and Lizard areas due to the impermeable nature of the underlying rock. This results in the development of many marshy areas known as wet flushes, that support moisture loving plants. There are several places where you should see the greater horsetail, an attractive, exotic looking plant that has long feathery branches and segmented flower stalks. On the coast proper look for the sturdy tree mallow, a tall plant with hairy stem and purple flowers.

④ Turn left at a T-junction just above the cove and again turn left where the path branches in about ¼ mile (400m) Continue along the cliff edge path to **Cadgwith**.

⑤ Follow a narrow path, signposted '**Coast Path**'. By a house gateway, go left up a surfaced path,

> **WHERE TO EAT AND DRINK** ⓘ
>
> The **Cadgwith Cove Inn** at Cadgwith has a good selection of pub food including some tasty crab soup and fresh mussels as well as pasties, baguettes and pizzas. The **Old Cellars Restaurant** in Cadgwith is licensed and features the courtyard of an old pilchard processing 'cellars' right opposite Cadgwith harbour beach. Morning coffee, lunch, afternoon tea with tasty home-made cakes, and evening meal. Fish and seafood specialities.

signposted '**Devil's Frying Pan**'. At an open area turn left, pass **Townplace Cottage**, cross a meadow and reach the **Devil's Frying Pan** itself.

⑥ At a junction, just past a chalet studio, follow a path inland to a T-junction with a rough track. Turn left and, at a public lane, go left again to reach the entrance to **Grade church**, after 1 mile (1.6km).

> **WHILE YOU'RE THERE** ⓘ
>
> The **Church of St Ruan** is a small, endearing building built mainly of local serpentine stone. It has a low tower, as if bitten off by the notorious Lizard wind. The east window is dedicated to Thomas Richard Collinson Harrison, a 16 year old who died in a cliff fall in 1909. Grade Church stands on raised ground above flood-prone fields. It is a raw, but atmospheric building that can be satisfyingly gloomy and primeval on dull days, and at dusk.

⑦ Follow the field edge behind the church, then cross the next field to reach a lane. **St Ruan's Well** is opposite diagonally left. Turn right for 200yds (183m), then branch off right between stone pillars to return to the **car park**.

Lifesavers at the Lizard

*A walk round Britain's most southerly point where coastwatchers,
lighthouse keepers and lifeboatmen stand guard.*

•DISTANCE•	6½ miles (10.4km)
•MINIMUM TIME•	4hrs
•ASCENT / GRADIENT•	220ft (67m) ▲▲▲
•LEVEL OF DIFFICULTY•	🚶 🚶 🚶
•PATHS•	Coastal footpaths, inland tracks and lanes. Please take note of path diversion notices at any erosion repair areas, 3 stiles
•LANDSCAPE•	Spectacular sea cliffs backed by open heathland
•SUGGESTED MAP•	aqua3 OS Explorer 103 The Lizard
•START / FINISH•	Grid reference: SW 703125
•DOG FRIENDLINESS•	Dogs on lead through grazed areas
•PARKING•	Large car park at centre of Lizard village. Donation box. Can be busy in summer
•PUBLIC TOILETS•	By car park at Lizard village

BACKGROUND TO THE WALK

Lizard Point's far south location can make it a place of sun and warmth although the sea is still in control here. For some distance offshore, reefs and sandbanks create massive 'overfalls' where, in stormy weather the sea becomes chaotic and dangerous. On the high ground of Lizard Point stands one of the most strategically important lighthouses in Britain. A coal-fired Lizard Lighthouse was built in 1619, but was short-lived, and it was not until 1752 that a more substantial lighthouse was built. It was first powered by coal and then, from 1812 onwards, by oil. Today's light uses electricity and has one of the most powerful beams in Britain.

Lifeboats

The route of the walk first leads to the picturesque Kynance Cove then winds its way along the coast path to Lizard Head and then to Lizard Point. In Polpeor Cove on the western side of Lizard Point, and seen clearly from the coast path, stands the disused lifeboat house of the old Lizard lifeboat. This was a bold location; the launching slipway faced into the teeth of southerly and westerly gales and too often it was impossible to launch the lifeboat, though epic missions were carried out over the years. In 1961 the lifeboat house was closed on the opening of a new lifeboat station at the more sheltered Kilcobben Cove near Landewednack's Church Cove to the east.

The Lizard was also famous for its connections with radio communications, a technology that has played its own crucial part in search and rescue at sea. East of Lizard Lighthouse, the route of the walk leads past the little wooden building of the old Marconi Wireless Station. From here, in 1901, the first wireless transmission was sent by Guglielmo Marconi. The letter 'S' in Morse code was sent from a, now demolished, 164ft (50m) aerial. It was received faintly – but almost immediately – over 2,000 miles (3,240km) away at St John's, Newfoundland, where the aerial had been attached to a kite. Within sight of the 'Marconi Bungalow', as the little building is called, is the ugly, white-painted building of the old Lloyds signal station on Bass Point. The original station was established in 1872 to take note of all shipping that passed the Lizard. In front of the Lloyds building is a one-time coastguard lookout that is now manned by members of the National Coastwatch Institution. Just over ½ mile (800m) further on is the spectacular location of the Lizard-Cadgwith Lifeboat station, the modern successor to lifeboats that were once stationed at Cadgwith, Church Cove, and Lizard Point. The record of service boards outside say everything about this ultimate expression of the service to mariners by local people over the years.

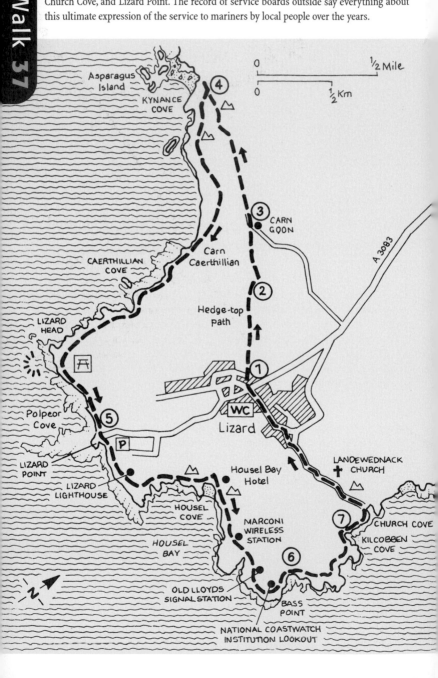

Walk 37 **Directions**

① Walk past the public toilets at the bottom end of the car park and go along a surfaced lane signed '**To Caerthillian and Kynance Coves**'. In 50yds (46m) bear right at a junction and go along a track, signed '**Public Footpath Kynance Cove**'. After a few paces, at a public footpath sign, bear off left behind a chalet and go up some steps, then follow a hedge-top path.

② Descend steps and go through a grove of privet. Negotiate two more sets of steps then bear slightly right across a field towards the just visible roof of a house. Go over a step stile to reach a surfaced road.

③ Follow the road past the house, called **Carn Goon**. In a few paces bear off right along a track. Reach a T-junction with a wide track and cross this to reach the bottom end of the National Trust car park for **Kynance Cove**. Pass in front of a National Trust information kiosk, then turn right and follow a track to Kynance Cove.

④ Walk back up from the cove to where a path goes off right, signed '**Coastal Path To Lizard Point**'. Follow a cobbled and stepped path steeply uphill, then continue along the coast path for about 1¼ miles (2km). Pass above **Pentreath Beach** and **Caerthillian Cove** and continue to the rocky **Lizard Head**

and then to **Lizard Point** and a car park and cafés.

⑤ Cross the car park and follow the coast path past the lighthouse. Descend steeply into **Housel Cove** and ascend just as steeply, ignoring a link path inland to **Lizard** village. Pass the old Marconi Wireless Station, at **Pen Olver**, the old Lloyds Signal Station and then the National Coastwatch Institution Lookout at **Bass Point**.

⑥ Follow a track past houses, then bear off right and follow the narrow coast path past **Hot Point** and on to the modern lifeboat house at **Kilcobben Cove**.

⑦ Go down steps on the far side of the lifeboat station and follow the coast path to **Church Cove**. Follow the public lane inland past **Landewednack Church** and continue steadily uphill to a junction with the main road on a bend beside a granite cross and a seat. Go left along **Beacon Terrace** to reach the **car park**.

WHERE TO EAT AND DRINK ⓘ

At Lizard Point car park the **Polpeor Café**, billed, with good reason as 'the Most Southerly Café in England' does a tasty selection of food including Cornish pasties, Cajun chicken and home made steak and kidney pies. Ice creams and drinks are also on sale. There are reduced opening hours in winter. You can eat and drink just by stepping off the coast path through the delightful cliff-side gardens of the **Housel Bay Hotel** on the east side of Housel Cove. A menu is posted alongside the path. Dogs are not allowed in the hotel and restaurant areas. The **Top House Inn** at Lizard village is an attractive and well-run, popular, traditional pub that has an excellent selection of bar meals as well as offering sandwiches of all types.

WHAT TO LOOK FOR ⓘ

Look for two garden escapees which thrive here. **Montbretia** (*Tritonia crocosmiflora*) has rich orange flowers, the **Hottentot fig** (*Carpobrutus edulis*) has large pink or yellow flowers and a wide-spreading mat of fleshy leaves.

Cliffs and Deep Woods at Portreath and Tehidy

A route along spectacular cliffs followed by a contrasting stroll through woods.

•DISTANCE•	4 miles (6.4km)
•MINIMUM TIME•	3hrs
•ASCENT / GRADIENT•	459ft (140m) ▲ ▲▲
•LEVEL OF DIFFICULTY•	🚶 🚶 🚶
•PATHS•	Good coastal path, woodland path, farm tracks
•LANDSCAPE•	Precipitous sea cliffs and deep woodland
•SUGGESTED MAP•	aqua3 OS Explorer 104 Redruth & St Agnes
•START / FINISH•	Grid reference: SW 656453
•DOG FRIENDLINESS•	Dogs on lead through grazed areas
•PARKING•	Portreath Beach
•PUBLIC TOILETS•	Portreath

BACKGROUND TO THE WALK

The sea cliffs near Portreath in Mid Cornwall, are made up of unstable shale and sandstone. Yet these are some of the most spectacular cliffs of all; their very friability lends itself to the formation of fantastic offshore islands and ridges of marginally harder rock. From the edge of the cliffs a flat platform of land, Carvannel Downs, once submerged beneath the sea, runs inland. It is a featureless landscape except where the dark curtain of Tehidy Woods breaks the profile. There can be no greater contrast than that between the bare, windswept cliffs and the enfolding trees, and this walk samples both environments.

Awesome Cliffs

The walk starts from Portreath's popular beach and harbour (▶ While You're There) and soon leads onto the awesome cliffs to the west of Portreath. You stroll along the edge of the flat, heath-covered Carvannel Downs aware always of the 260ft (80m) cliffs only a few steps away. Below lie vast rock islands dotting the inaccessible sands of Western Cove. The Horse is a breathtaking ridge of rock and grass that projects from the cliff face and makes up the east wall of Ralph's Cupboard, a vast dizzying gulf that belies the quaintness of its name and that is said to be the remains of a huge cavern whose roof collapsed. Do not be tempted to go too near the edge of the cliffs, however, especially in windy weather. Far ahead you can see Godrevy Lighthouse on its rocky island.

Beyond Ralph's Cupboard, a name that may derive from a one-time smuggler, or from an old Cornish word, the path leads steeply down into Porth-cadjack Cove. Here a thin stream of water pours over the lower cliff edge and 19th-century smugglers used to hoist their contraband from the beach using elaborate pulley-systems. Beyond, above Basset's Cove, the route turns inland and draws you into the enfolding trees of Tehidy Woods, once the estate of the Basset family who were famous mine owners. The Bassets planted extensive woodlands around their Georgian house and these now mature woods still offer shelter and security after the exhilarating exposure of the cliffs. Countless paths wriggle through the trees, but in such Hansel and Gretel territory, it is best to keep to the route back to Portreath.

Portreath

GLENFEADON TERRACE

① P

FEADON FARM

⑧

PORTREATH BEACH

Western Hill

② BATTERY HILL

Old Mineral Tramway incline

⑦

Western Cove

The Horse

RALPH'S CUPBOARD

Carvannel Downs

⑥

PORTH-CADJACK COVE

GOLF COURSE

⑤

BASSET'S COVE

P ③ ④ TEHIDY COUNTRY PARK

Ornamental lakes

CRANE CASTLE

Crane Islands

C

TEHIDY WOODS

Tehidy Park House (Private)

Kennels' Hill signpost

GREENBANK COVE

RESKAJEAGE DOWNS

DEADMAN'S COVE

Ⓐ

Ⓑ DOWNS FARM

COOMBE

N

½ Mile

0

0   1Km

Walk 38

Walk 38 Directions

① Turn right outside the **Portreath Beach car park**, cross a bridge and turn right up **Battery Hill**, signposted 'Coast Path'. Follow the lane uphill and on to where it ends at houses above the beach. Go left in front of garages, signposted '**North Coast Foot Path**'.

② Follow the path through a gate and keep straight uphill to the cliff top. Don't go too close to the cliff edge. Turn left to reach a wooden gate, then follow the path round the cliff edge above **Ralph's Cupboard**. Continue by steep paths into and out of **Porth-cadjack Cove**.

③ Reach a car parking area above **Basset Cove**. Follow the broad track inland, then at the public road, cross over and turn left for 40yds (37m); watch out for fast traffic. Reach a granite grid stile on the right. Cross the stile, then follow a narrow path into **Tehidy Woods**.

④ Keep straight ahead at a crossing. Soon pass a right-hand junction, and then a left-hand

---

WHILE YOU'RE THERE ⓘ

Portreath harbour and docks still give some idea of their industrial past. The original fishing cove was turned into a harbour in the 1760s. Copper ore from the mines at Camborne and Redruth was exported from here. By the 1830s a railway connected Portreath with Hayle and the mines. You can see the lower section of a steep incline plane, on the south side of the valley. The last part of the walk passes beneath this incline. Sectioned bays full of coal, limestone, ore and stone once occupied the land behind the harbour where modern houses now stand. The 'pepperpot' north of the harbour was a navigational guide.

---

junction, signposted '**Pedestrians Only**'. Keep straight ahead to reach a T-junction with a broad track. Turn left.

⑤ Reach a junction and four-way signpost beside two seats. (A café can be reached in ¼ mile (400m) down the right-hand signposted track.) On the main route, keep straight on, signposted '**East Lodge**'. Reach a junction by a seat. Go right and go through a wooden kissing gate. Eyes left here before crossing to check for keen golfers about to tee-off. Go through a metal kissing gate and follow the track alongside the golf course.

⑥ About 40yds (37m) beyond the end of the golf course section, bear off left into woods by a staggered wooden barrier, signposted '**Pedestrians Only**'. Stay on the main path, ignoring side paths, then bear round right to a small car park and to a public road. Cross diagonally right and then go left between wooden posts with red marks. Follow the often muddy track ahead.

⑦ Go right onto a wider track by a field gate. The next section can be extremely muddy during wet weather. Pass holiday chalets and reach a T-junction above farm buildings at **Feadon Farm**.

⑧ Turn left, then in a few paces turn right down a concrete track. At a farmyard go sharp left by a public footpath sign and follow a path down through woods to reach a surfaced road. Just past '**Glenfeadon Castle**' turn left along **Glenfeadon Terrace**, pass beneath a bridge, then at a junction keep ahead along **Tregea Terrace** and back to **Portreath Beach car park**.

To Deadman's Cove

The coast path continues beyond Basset's Cove in spectacular style.
See map and information panel for Walk 38

•DISTANCE•	7 miles (11.3km)
•MINIMUM TIME•	4hrs
•ASCENT / GRADIENT•	Negligible ▲▲ ▲ ▲
•LEVEL OF DIFFICULTY•	🚶 🚶 🚶

Walk 39 Directions
(Walk 38 option)

This longer version of Walk 38 continues along the cliff tops past **Basset's Cove** at Point ③ on the Walk 38. Keep straight across the bottom edge of the car parking area and keep on following the coast path. Inevitably, the cliffs at Basset's Cove were exploited for building stone – there were few places that escaped the resilient determination of the Cornish to survive through hard work. The coast path leads easily on from here, past the vestigial remains of a 'cliff castle' or promontory fort called **Crane Castle**. You can still make out the banks and ditch that fortified the settlement on the landward side, but the once substantial promontory, that may even have incorporated the offshore islands seen from here, has long since collapsed into the sea. A short distance further on, at the edge of **Reskajeage Downs**, cliff collapse and landslide are even more evident above **Greenbank Cove**, where you can see the folded terraces of a landslip piled below you. A spectacular path winds its way down this tumbled landscape to the quiet beach below.

Just beyond Greenbank Cove and the cheerfully-named **Deadman's Cove**, you reach a small car parking area, Point Ⓐ, close to the public road. Go inland to the road here and cross it with care, then go over a stile and follow the edge of a field downhill and on between thorn trees. This path leads to a road at **Downs Farm** where you turn left for about 130yds (120m). On a right hand bend at **Coombe**, bear off left and follow a path past a cottage. Follow a tree-shrouded path ahead to merge with a track into the **Tehidy Country Park** at Point Ⓑ. Follow the broad drive through the trees ahead, then at a junction, turn left and reach a T-junction at **Kennels' Hill** signpost, Point Ⓒ. Turn right here, signposted '**East Lodge**' and follow the broad track to reach a junction with a track coming in from the left at Point ⑤ on Walk 38.

WHERE TO EAT AND DRINK ⓘ

There is a café at the south entrance to **Tehidy Woods**. Follow the sign from Point ⑤ on Walk 38 or by diverting to the lakes to reach Point ⑤ from Point Ⓒ on Walk 39. In **Portreath** the **Beach Café** does drinks and snacks and the **Pirates Retreat** on the inner edge of the car park offers fish and chips. The **Basset Arms** is on the south side of the river and is passed at the end of the walk.

Walk 40

From Helston to Porthleven by Loe Bar

A walk through the National Trust property of Penrose, between the peaceful lake known as the Loe and the restless sea.

•DISTANCE•	5 miles (8km)
•MINIMUM TIME•	2hrs 30min
•ASCENT / GRADIENT•	82ft (25m) ▲▲ ▲ ▲
•LEVEL OF DIFFICULTY•	🚶 🚶 🚶
•PATHS•	Excellent paths and estate tracks
•LANDSCAPE•	Densely vegetated river valley, poolside woods and open, sandy coast
•SUGGESTED MAP•	aqua3 OS Explorer 103 The Lizard
•START / FINISH•	Grid reference: SW 656272
•DOG FRIENDLINESS•	Dogs strictly on the lead within Penrose Park area. No dogs on Loe Bar and beach from Easter to September
•PARKING•	Penrose Amenity Area car park, Helston. Turn off the A394 onto the B3304 at the large roundabouts on the outskirts of Helston. Car park is 200yds (183m) along the road on the left, opposite a boating pool and next to a garage
•PUBLIC TOILETS•	Porthleven
•NOTE•	Buses 2 and 2A, Helston–Porthleven, about 14 times a day

Walk 40 Directions

This undemanding walk leads from below the town of Helston to the fishing village of Porthleven, via the valley of the River Cober and the remarkable Loe, the largest natural freshwater lake in Cornwall. What makes the Loe exceptional is that its southern end is separated from the sea by a sand bar, known as Loe Bar. The Loe's name derives simply from the Cornish word *logh*, meaning 'pool'. The Loe evolved in medieval times from its origins as the estuary of the River Cober because of a build-up of silt washed down from the countless tin and copper mines inland. The silt added its weight to encroaching shingle spits at the seaward end of the

estuary and by the 13th century, a formidable dam, or 'bar', of sand and shingle separated the pool from the sea. The Loe is as deep as 30ft (9m) at its seaward end.

Until the middle of the 19th century Loe Bar was regularly breached by gangs of diggers to ease flooding in the Cober valley below Helston. The rush of water out of the pool is said to have left a thin

---

WHERE TO EAT AND DRINK ℹ

Porthleven has several pubs, restaurants and cafés. The **Crab Pot Restaurant** serves breakfast, morning coffee, lunches, cream teas and evening meals. The **Harbour Inn** is a long-established harbourside pub with a pleasing atmosphere, good food and a fine selection of beers.

Walk 40

WHAT TO LOOK FOR ⓘ

The Loe is a sanctuary for birds including moorhen, mallard, teal and mute swan. Most of these are winter visitors, but some mallard and moorhen nest here and there is always something to see. Ospreys have been known to stop off at the Loe for a taste of the lake's trout. Look for cormorants and herons that often perch in the Monterey pines just inland from the Bar. Aside from birds, there are many exotic shrubs within the Penrose estate. Near Bar Lodge look for the bright red spiky leaves and blue flower of *Fascicularia pitcairniifolia*, a member of the pineapple family.

yellow stain for miles offshore. Today, modern flood release systems alleviate the problem of flooding and the Loe has become a splendid reserve for wildlife, while the Bar makes for a dramatic flourish between peaceful pool and restless Atlantic. The Loe lies within the **Penrose Estate**, ancestral home from the late 12th to the late 18th century of the Penrose family and then of the Rogers family who gave the estate to the National Trust in 1974. Today the Trust maintains the landscaping and carriageways established in the 18th century and has created a network of paths for the enjoyment of the public. The walk begins at the public car park beside the Penrose Amenity Area to the south west of Helston.

At the far end of the car park go through a gap to the left of the '**Penrose Amenity Area**' sign and then turn right along a concrete drive, past a National Trust sign, '**Lower Nansloe**'. In about ½ mile (800m) pass an old chimney stack, the remains of the 18th-century **Castle Wary** lead and silver mine. In 50yds (46m) turn right through a wooden gate, then cross a sturdy causeway that was built in 1987.

Dogs must be kept on the lead here. You are now at the heart of the almost subtropical **Loe Marsh**, the choked gut of the **River Cober**, dense with alder and willow trees and moisture-loving plants. On the other side of the causeway, go through another gate, then turn left along a wide drive through the **Oak Grove**. Soon you pass a bird hide in a fine location for viewing the reedy shores of the **Loe**.

Reach the Victorian **Helston Lodge**, go through a gate, then follow the drive to where it forks. Take the left fork. There is a fine view of **Penrose House** from here; the house is a private dwelling. Continue past the old stable block and on alongside the Loe. The old carriageway that you are following leads through **Bar Walk Plantation** to **Bar Lodge** above **Loe Bar**. You can reach the Bar from here, but although you may feel tempted to swim from the sandy shore, or from the long stretch of beach, **Porthleven Sands**, that runs all the way to **Porthleven**, take heed of the warning notices; the ground shelves steeply close to shore here and there are dangerous tidal currents. Porthleven is a delightful destination, a traditional Cornish harbour of great character.

WHILE YOU'RE THERE ⓘ

Stroll across **Loe Bar** up to the **Anson Memorial** on its south eastern side. This simple stone cross commemorates the loss of the 44-gun frigate *Anson*, wrecked on Loe Bar in 1807. Over 100 sailors drowned, many of them as they tried to struggle ashore through the surf. Those on the beach could do nothing to save them, but the frustration of one local man Henry Trengrouse led him to devote his life to developing a rocket apparatus that became standard life saving equipment for coastguards.

Walk 41

Wildflower Haven at Mullion

The heathland of the Lizard Peninsula supports some of the most remarkable of Britain's wild flowers.

•DISTANCE•	7 miles (11.3km)
•MINIMUM TIME•	4hrs
•ASCENT / GRADIENT•	164ft (50m) ▲ ▲ ▲
•LEVEL OF DIFFICULTY•	🚶 🚶 🚶
•PATHS•	Good inland tracks and paths, can be muddy in places during wet weather. Coastal footpath, 21 stiles
•LANDSCAPE•	Flat heathland and high sea cliff
•SUGGESTED MAP•	aqua3 OS Explorer 103 The Lizard
•START / FINISH•	Grid reference: SW 669162
•DOG FRIENDLINESS•	Dogs on lead through grazed areas. Notices indicate
•PARKING•	Predannack Wollas Farm car park (National Trust)
•PUBLIC TOILETS•	Mullion Cove, 200yds (183m) up road from harbour

BACKGROUND TO THE WALK

The heathland of the Lizard Peninsula near Mullion lacks the rugged beauty of Cornwall's granite moors; its flatness seems a dull contrast to the dramatic sea cliffs that define its edges; the only punctuation marks are the huge satellite dishes of the nearby Goonhilly tracking station and the lazily revolving blades of modern wind turbines. Yet, beneath the skin, this seemingly featureless landscape is botanically unique and exciting, not least because the Lizard's calcareous soil is rich in magnesium and supports plants that are more often seen in chalk or limestone regions. The warming influence of the sea and the area's generally mild and frost-free climate encourages growth.

Famous Plant

The Lizard's most famous plant is the Cornish heath, rare in Britain generally, but abundant on the Lizard. In full bloom it contributes to a glorious mosaic of colour, its pink and white flowers matched by the brilliant yellow of Western gorse and the deeper pinks of cross-leaved heath and bell heather. From the very start of the walk you are at the heart of the heathland. More common plants include spring squill, thrift and foxglove. Deeper into the heath are a variety of orchids including the rare green winged orchid, with its purple-lipped flowers.

Soapy Cove

Near the turning point of the walk you pass close to the old wartime Predannack airfield from where modern gliders soar into the air. Soon, the route joins the coast at Gew Graze, a feature that is also known as 'Soapy Cove' because of the presence of steatite, or soapstone. This is a fairly rare type of rock which was once used in the 18th-century production of china and porcelain. The final part of the route, along the cliffs to Mullion Cove, brings more flower spotting opportunities. On the path out of Gew Graze look for the yellow bracts and purple florets of carline thistle; the straw-coloured bracts curl over the flowerheads to protect them in wet weather.

Another remarkable plant is thyme broomrape, a dark reddish-brown, almost dead-looking plant that obtains its chlorophyll as a parasite growing on thyme. Such plants are often difficult to spot, whereas the smooth grassy slopes of the cliff tops near Mullion are a riot of powder blue spring squill, white sea campion and the yellow heads of lesser celandine and kidney vetch.

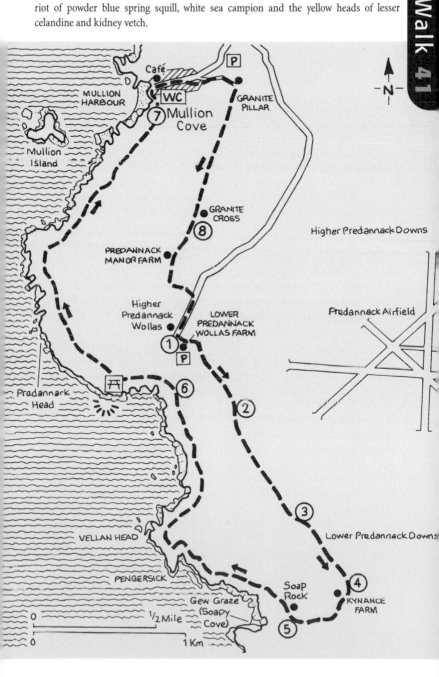

Walk 41

Walk 41 Directions

① Leave **Predannack Wollas Farm** car park by its bottom end. Follow the winding track ahead for just under ½ mile (800m) to where it ends at a gate. (Ignore a signposted track going off left just before this gate.) Beyond the gate, bear left to a stile. Follow the edge of the next field to a stile, then continue to open ground by a gate in a fence on the right.

② Go over the stile next to the gate, then bear away at an angle from the fence along a path to reach English Nature's **Kynance Farm Nature Reserve**. Keep ahead towards distant buildings.

③ Watch for a gap in the hedge on the left, go through the gap, then cross the next field to reach a rough track. Turn right along the track for a few paces then bear off left and follow the edge of the scrub.

④ Go through a gate, then follow a track going right. Merge with another track, and then in a few paces, and just before a ford, bear off to the right along a track towards the coast (**Kynance Farm** is up to the right).

⑤ At a crossing with the coast path, go right and steeply uphill, then go over a stile onto the cliff top. Follow the coast path as it winds round the edge of the often projecting cliffs at **Pengersick** and **Vellan Head**.

⑥ Go left at a junction, just past a National Trust sign for '**Predannack**'. (You can return to the car park by following the inland path from here.) Cross a stream in a dip and climb up left and continue along the coast path to **Mullion Cove** and Harbour.

⑦ Go up the road from **Mullion Harbour** and just beyond the public toilets and the shop, turn off right at a coast path sign. Keep to the right of the entrance to a holiday residential site and follow a track uphill. On a bend and just before a granite pillar, go off right and over a stone stile. Follow the path ahead through a grove of thorn trees and then through fields.

⑧ Pass a tall granite cross and then reach a lane and turn right along the lane towards the farm. Just before **Predannack Manor Farm** entrance, go left over a stile by a field gate, then turn right along the field edge. Go over a stile, then left along a hedged-in path, cross a stile and cross two fields to reach a lane (watch for traffic). Turn right to **Predannack Wollas Farm** car park.

WHILE YOU'RE THERE ⓘ

Spend some time at **Mullion Harbour**. The harbour dates from the 1890s and is built like a little fortress for the good reason that the cove's position on the eastern shore of Mount's Bay leaves it open to the most ferocious storms from the west and south west. This western coast of the Lizard Peninsula was always known as a 'wrecking shore', especially in the days of sail when vessels rounding the opposite 'horn' of the bay, Land's End, could easily become 'embayed' if they did not set course properly to clear the Lizard. Once embayed in onshore storms, a sailing vessel was easily driven ashore. Mullion Harbour gave shelter to pilchard, crab and lobster fishing boats.

WHERE TO EAT AND DRINK ⓘ

There is a café at Mullion Harbour, the **Porthmellin Café**, serving full cooked breakfast, morning coffee, cream teas, crab sandwiches, ice creams and soft drinks. Open Easter to September.

The Smuggler King of Prussia Cove

A pleasant stroll through the coastal domain of one of Cornwall's most famous smugglers.

•DISTANCE•	4 miles (6.4km)
•MINIMUM TIME•	3hrs
•ASCENT / GRADIENT•	394ft (120m) ▲▲▲
•LEVEL OF DIFFICULTY•	👫 👫 👫
•PATHS•	Good field paths and coastal paths, 18 stiles
•LANDSCAPE•	Quiet coast and countryside
•SUGGESTED MAP•	aqua3 OS Explorer 102 Land's End
•START / FINISH•	Grid reference: SW 554282
•DOG FRIENDLINESS•	Dogs on lead through grazed areas
•PARKING•	Trenalls, Prussia Cove. Small, privately-owned car park. Or car park at Perranuthnoe, from where the walk can be started at Point ⑤
•PUBLIC TOILETS•	Perranuthnoe

BACKGROUND TO THE WALK

Smuggling clings to the image of Cornwall like the Atlantic mist through which the old time 'freetraders' so often stole ashore with their cargoes of tea, spirits, tobacco, silk, china and even playing cards. Modern smuggling, chiefly of drugs, has no such romantic sheen, while nostalgia blurs the record of incidental brutality that often accompanied 18th-century smuggling. Yet we will not be robbed of our romance, and, in truth, the image of honest adventuring that we attach so eagerly to old time smuggling is often borne out by that same record.

Mount's Bay

Such 'honest adventuring' seems personified by the famous Carter family who lived at Prussia Cove on the eastern shores of Mount's Bay in West Cornwall. The cove is really more of a series of rocky inlets close to the magnificent St Michael's Mount, the castle-crowned island that so enhances the inner corner of Mount's Bay. John and Henry (Harry) Carter were the best known members of the family and ran their late 18th-century smuggling enterprise with great flair and efficiency. They even fortified the headland overlooking Prussia Cove in a move that echoed the defensive settlements of the Celtic Iron Age. John Carter was the more flamboyant, styling himself in early childhood games as 'the King of Prussia' an indication of contemporary awareness of the activities of Fredrick the Great of Prussia. The name stuck and the original Porth Leah Cove became known as the 'King of Prussia's Cove'. Fame indeed. John Carter had integrity. He once broke in to an excise store in Penzance to recover smuggled goods confiscated from Prussia Cove in his absence. The authorities knew it must have been Carter because they said he was 'an upright man' and took only his own goods. His brother Harry became a Methodist preacher and forbade swearing on all his vessels.

Remoteness

The nature of the coast and countryside around Prussia Cove says everything about the environment within which smuggling flourished. As you follow the route of the walk inland, you can sense the remoteness of hamlet and cottage still, the secretiveness of the lanes and paths that wriggle inland from a coast that is formidable, yet accessible to skilled seamen. At Perranuthnoe, the narrow, flat beach resounds with the sound of the sea where modern surfers and holidaymakers now enjoy themselves. From here the coastal footpath leads back along the coast across the rocky headland of Cudden Point to where a series of secluded coves make up the Carter's old kingdom of Prussia Cove.

Walk 42 Directions

① From the car park entrance walk back along the approach road, past the large house. Watch for traffic. After the second bend, by the camp site entrance, look for a stile on the left, just past a field gate.

② Cross the stile and follow the field edge, bearing off to the right, where it bends left, to reach a stile in the hedge opposite. Walk down the edge of the next field, behind **Acton Castle** (private dwellings), then turn right along field edges to a stile into the adjacent rough lane. Turn right.

③ Turn left along a rough track at a junction in front of a bungalow entrance at **Trevean Farm**. At a left-hand bend go onto a stony track for just a few paces, then when you come to a public footpath sign, ascend to the right, up some narrow steps, then turn left along the edge of the field.

WHILE YOU'RE THERE ⓘ
Take time midway in the walk to enjoy **Perranuthnoe Beach**, known as Perran Sands, a fine little beach that is south-facing and catches the sun all day. It's also worth exploring **Prussia Cove** itself, and its individual rocky inlets. This is a good place for a swim at low tide in the crystal clear water.

---

④ At **Trebarvah**, cross the farm lane, pass in front of some barns, (there's a view of **St Michael's Mount** ahead), then follow a field edge to a hedged-in path. Follow the path ahead through fields, then pass in front of some houses to reach the main road opposite the **Victoria Inn**. Go left and follow the road to the car park above **Perranuthnoe Beach**.

⑤ For the beach and **Cabin Café**, (▶ Where to Eat and Drink) keep straight ahead. On the main route of the walk, go left, just beyond the car park, and along a lane. Bear right at a fork, then bear right again just past a house at a junction.

WHERE TO EAT AND DRINK ⓘ
The **Victoria Inn** at Perranuthnoe is conveniently located midway on the walk. The pub has a good selection of beers and other drinks and also does excellent bar meals. On the approach to Perranuthnoe Beach is the busy little **Cabin Café**, open all summer and at week-ends in winter.

WHAT TO LOOK FOR ⓘ
Along the sandy paths and fields east of Perranuthnoe, the feathery-leafed tamarisk (*Tamarix anglica*), lends an exotic Mediterranean atmosphere to the Cornish scene. The tamarisk was introduced to Britain from the Mediterranean and is often used at coastal locations as a windbreak because of its resilience and its ability to survive the battering of salt-laden winds.

---

⑥ Go down a track towards the sea and follow it round left. Then, at a field entrance, go down right (signposted), turn sharp left through a gap and follow the coast path along the edge of **Trebarvah** and **Stackhouse Cliffs**.

⑦ At the National Trust property of **Cudden Point**, follow the path steeply uphill and then across the inner slope of the headland above **Piskies Cove**.

⑧ Go through a gate and pass some ancient fishing huts. Follow the path round the edge of the **Bessy's Cove** inlet of **Prussia Cove**, to reach a track by a thatched cottage. The cove can be reached down a path on the right just before this junction. Turn right and follow the track, keeping left at junctions, to return to the **car park** at the start of the walk.

Church Paths and Coastguard Ways at St Ives

A long walk that follows old paths once used when people travelled on foot out of necessity.

•DISTANCE•	8 miles (12.9km)
•MINIMUM TIME•	3hrs
•ASCENT / GRADIENT•	394ft (120m) ▲▲ ▲ ▲
•LEVEL OF DIFFICULTY•	🚶 🚶 🚶
•PATHS•	Coastal path, can be quite rocky. Field paths, some stiles
•LANDSCAPE•	Very scenic coast and small inland fields
•SUGGESTED MAP•	aqua3 OS Explorer 102 Land's End
•START / FINISH•	Grid reference: SW 522408
•DOG FRIENDLINESS•	Dogs on lead through grazed areas
•PARKING•	Upper Trenwith car park St Ives or Porthmeor Beach
•PUBLIC TOILETS•	Smeaton's Pier and Porthmeor car park

BACKGROUND TO THE WALK

In the days before better transport, the scenic road from St Ives to St Just, along the north coast of the Land's End Peninsula, was no more than a rough track used for carrying heavier loads by cart and wagon, horse or donkey. Even before this track evolved people travelled more easily on foot along the coastal belt below the hills, through what is still a palimpsest of ancient fields, first carved out by Bronze and Iron Age farmers. Until the early 20th century the field paths, with their marvellous punctuation marks of granite stiles, were used by local people to visit each other and to travel to church and to the market at St Ives.

Mosaic

The coastal paths on the outer edge of this wonderful mosaic of ancient fields barely existed in earlier times. They were useful only to individual farms directly inland and were often mere links between paths down to isolated coves. As commerce and foreign wars increased, the coastline of South West England especially, came under much closer scrutiny by the authorities. When 19th-century smuggling was at its height, government 'revenue men' patrolled as best they could the wilder reaches of the coast to foil the 'freetraders'. In later years the coastguard service also patrolled the coast on foot until there were few sections that were not passable, by footpath at least. Linking these paths to create a continuous route for the leisure walker was the final stage in the evolution of today's coastal footpath.

This walk starts from the maritime heart of St Ives and heads west along the glorious coastline, once watched so assiduously by coastguards and excisemen. This is a very remote and wild part of the West Cornwall coast, a landscape of exquisite colours in spring and summer and where the steep and vegetated cliffs are not breached until the narrow Treveal Valley breaks through to the sea at River Cove. Here the route turns inland and plunges instantly into a lush, green countryside that seems, at times, far removed from the sea. Field paths lead unswervingly back towards St Ives with a sequence of granite stiles reminding you of a very different world when this journey was an everyday event for Cornish folk.

PORTHGWIDDEN BEACH

ST IVES MUSEUM

SMEATON'S PIER

NATIONAL COASTWATCH LOOKOUT

The Island

CHAPEL OF ST NICHOLAS

PORTHMEOR BEACH

CARRICK DU

CLODGY POINT

HOR POINT

HELLESVEOR CLIFF

TROWAN FARM

TREVALGAN FARM

BURTHALLAN LANE

ST IVES

WC

WC

P

① ② ③ ④ ⑤ ⑥ ⑦ ⑧ ⑨ ⑩ ⑪ ⑫

RIVER COVE

TREVAIL MILL

N

0   ½ Mile

0   1 Km

Walk 43 Directions

① Walk along the harbour front towards **Smeaton's Pier**. Just before the pier entrance, turn left up **Sea View Place**. Where the road bends, keep straight on into **Wheal Dream**. Turn right past **St Ives Museum**, then follow a walkway to **Porthgwidden Beach**.

② Cross the car park above the beach and climb to the **National Coastwatch lookout**. Go down steps, behind the building at the back of the lookout, then follow a footway to **Porthmeor Beach**. Go along the beach up to the car park.

③ Go up steps beside the public toilets, then turn right along a surfaced track past bowling and putting greens. Continue to the rocky headlands of **Carrick Du** and **Clodgy Point**.

④ From the distinctive square-cut rock on **Clodgy Point** walk uphill and through a low wall. Follow the path round to the right and across a boggy area. In about ½ mile (800m) go left at a junction.

⑤ Reach a T-junction with a track just past a National Trust sign,

'**Hellesveor Cliff**'. Turn right and follow the coast path. (The short version of this walk goes left and inland from here.)

⑥ Keep right at a junction just past an old mine stack and shed on the left. Continue to **River Cove**. On the other side of the Cove, go left at a junction and head inland through shady woods.

⑦ At a junction with a track, go left over a cattle grid, then follow signs past **Trevail Mill**. Go through a metal gate and climb steadily.

⑧ Cross a track and follow the hedged-in path opposite. In about 50yds (46m) go left over a stile by a black and white pole. Follow field edges ahead over intervening stiles.

⑨ Follow the right-hand edge of the field containing a parish boundary stone. Cross two stiles and at a hedge corner, bear right across the field and continue to **Trevalgan Farm**. Cross behind the farm to a stile, then continue to Trowan Farm.

⑩ At **Trowan Farm**, go left over a stile in front of a house, then turn right. Go through the farmyard to a lane, then turn left, then right, over a stile. Follow the field paths over several stiles.

⑪ Go over a stile and through a metal gate, pass a field gap, then go left and down a hedged-in path. Go over a big stile and pass between high hedges to reach a lane.

⑫ Turn right along the lane (**Burthallan Lane**) to a T-junction with the main road. Turn left and follow the road downhill to **Porthmeor Beach** and the car park.

WHILE YOU'RE THERE   ⓘ

At the start of the walk the **St Ives Museum** is a delightfully venerable institution portraying the history and culture of St Ives with some panache. Above Porthmeor Beach is the splendid **Tate Gallery St Ives**, a custom-built gallery celebrating the work of the mainly Modernist St Ives painters. There is a café within the gallery building. No dogs, other than guide dogs, are allowed inside the gallery, but visitors often leave their dogs secured at the entrance rotunda.

The Chapel of St Nicholas and Hor Point

A short option takes you out to the little chapel on the headland.
See map and information panel for Walk 43

•DISTANCE•	3½ miles (5.7km)
•MINIMUM TIME•	1hr 30min
•ASCENT / GRADIENT•	295ft (90m) ▲▲ ▲ ▲
•LEVEL OF DIFFICULTY•	🚶 🚶 🚶

Walk 44 Directions (Walk 43 option)

This shorter walk follows the main route from **St Ives Harbour**. As you climb over the Island, Point ②, divert to the little **Chapel of St Nicholas**, on the summit. The chapel dates from the 16th century when it was used, not only as a seaman's chapel but also as an early form of lighthouse. In later years it was used as a lookout by revenue men on the watch for smugglers. Follow the main walk past the rocky headlands of **Carrick Du** and **Clodgy Point** and continue round the edge of the cliffs to Point ⑤, where this shortened version of the walk turns inland.

The headland just ahead of this junction is **Hor Point**. In the 1950s, long before public consciousness was quite so attuned to environmentalism, St Ives Council put forward plans to use **Hor Point** for tipping rubbish. This reflected the traditional attitude of earlier generations that wilderness sea cliffs were out of sight and out of mind and were thus exploitable for everything from quarrying to

rubbish disposal. (Also around this time a proposal to site a nuclear power station on the beautiful **Zennor Moors**, above the coast, was rejected.) Hor Point was saved from spoliation because the landowner, faced with potential compulsory purchase of the point by the council, sold it instead to the National Trust and the rubbish tip plan was soon shelved.

With the preserved beauty of the coast and moors in mind, you turn inland at Point ⑤, to follow a hedged-in track that is probably centuries-old. Such tracks gave access to the cliff, where animals were grazed and where stone was gathered for building and furze for fuel. At Point Ⓑ turn left onto the main route and follow the last part of the old field path back to **St Ives**.

WHERE TO EAT AND DRINK ⓘ

There are no refreshment points on the route once you leave St Ives, but the town has numerous pubs, restaurants and takeaways. The **Sloop Inn**, midway along the harbour front, is a famous harbourside inn that does pub food and is usually very busy. Just past the Sloop is the **Cornish Pasty Shop** where you can buy delicious pasties. Further along is **Caffè Pasta**, a good restaurant.

Branching Out to St Ives

Following the coastal footpath alongside the scenic St Ives railway line above the golden beaches of St Ives Bay.

•DISTANCE•	4 miles (6.4km)
•MINIMUM TIME•	3hrs
•ASCENT / GRADIENT•	180ft (55m) ▲ ▲ ▲
•LEVEL OF DIFFICULTY•	🚶 🚶 🚶
•PATHS•	Excellent
•LANDSCAPE•	Coastal sand dunes, cliff paths and surfaced tracks
•SUGGESTED MAP•	aqua3 OS Explorer 102 Land's End
•START•	Grid reference: SW 544365
•FINISH•	Grid reference: SW 521402
•DOG FRIENDLINESS•	Can let dogs off lead. Summer dog bans on Carbis Bay Beach and Porthminster Beach
•PARKING•	Station car park, St Ives, or Park-and-Ride car park, Lelant Saltings. Large car park with attendant; expensive. Or park at St Ives Station Pay-and-Display car park, catch a train to Lelant Saltings and walk back to St Ives
•PUBLIC TOILETS•	At Lelant Saltings, Carbis Bay and Porthminster Beach
•NOTE•	This walk uses the Penzance–St Erth–St Ives railway. In summer about 20 trains a day run between Penzance, St Erth and St Ives, stopping at Lelant Saltings, Lelant and Carbis Bay. Fewer trains stop at Lelant Halt and some of these are by request only. Check timetables carefully

Walk 45 Directions

In 1877 the archetypal Cornish fishing village of St Ives was linked to the main line railway and was never the same again. The 4½ miles (7.2km) of track that wound its way from St Erth along the estuary of the River Hayle and then above St Ives Bay, was intended to make markets more accessible to the local fishing industry. It also opened the town to the fast-developing tourism of the late 19th century. Fishing declined, but by the 1940s and 1950s the branch line was carrying tens of thousands of holidaymaking families to St Ives and was enjoyed by huge numbers of local people.

Today the line carries crowds of day-visitors and its scenic qualities are still unspoiled. An added bonus is that the beautiful surroundings through which the line passes are also traversed by the coastal footpath. You can travel either way between station halts and return on foot through magnificent coastal scenery. There are three Halts on the line and the walk described starts at **Lelant Saltings Halt**, where there is a large car park.

Look for a gap in the hedge, opposite the car park toilets and pay kiosk and beside a **Park-and-Ride** sign. Go through the gap, then turn right along a surfaced lane, past houses with colourful gardens,

Walk 45

to reach **Lelant Halt** in under
½ mile (800m). Continue along the
tree-shaded lane and in just under
¼ mile (400m) reach a T-junction.
Turn up right to the **Church of St
Uny and St Anta**. To the left of the
churchyard entrance follow an
obvious footpath that leads across
the **West Cornwall Golf Course**.
Look out for flying golf balls. Turn
down right beside a concrete
blockhouse, go under the railway
bridge, then turn left by a house at
a coast path sign.

The way now leads above the sand
dunes of **Porth Kidney** where a
glittering expanse of sand is
exposed at low tide. Soon you climb
steadily between hedges to the
headland of **Carrack Gladden**, or
Hawke's Point. Just past a railway
crossing you have a choice of
routes. Keeping to the higher route
leads alongside the railway to
Carbis Bay Halt, but for a more
scenic route take the right-hand
branch steeply downhill and along
the grassy cliff edge, to reach the
road where you turn down right to
Carbis Bay beach and the promise
of a swim in warm weather. Follow
the track in front of the **Carbis Bay
Hotel**, then turn up left to reach a
footbridge across the railway.
Follow the path ahead and on along
a surfaced lane that runs through a
residential area. Where the lane
branches, keep straight ahead,

signposted '**Coast Path**'. You soon
reach a marvellous relic of old
St Ives, the **Baulking House**. This
historic building, with its flanking
shelters, was used during the

traditional pilchard fishing of the
19th and early 20th centuries. From
here a lookout, called a '*huer*', kept
watch for the tell-tale purple stain
of pilchard shoals in the bay below.
The huer would then use hand-held
signalling devices to direct the
seine-net boats in the silent, skilful
enclosing of the shoal. Just past the
Baulking House keep straight across
at a crossroads and follow a track
past blue-painted seats. Where the
track bends sharply right, keep
ahead past the final seat and go
down a narrow path, and then some
steps, to reach **Porthminster Beach**.
Walk past the line of beach huts to
reach **St Ives Station** and car park,
or continue into the town itself.

Merry Maidens and the Way Down to Lamorna

A coastal and inland walk from the picturesque Lamorna Cove, passing an ancient stone circle on the way.

·DISTANCE·	6 miles (9.7km)
·MINIMUM TIME·	3hrs 30min
·ASCENT / GRADIENT·	558ft (170m) ▲▲▲
·LEVEL OF DIFFICULTY·	👫 👫 👫
·PATHS·	Good coastal footpaths, field paths and rocky tracks
·LANDSCAPE·	Picturesque coastline, fields and wooded valleys. 7 stiles
·SUGGESTED MAP·	aqua3 OS Explorer 102 Land's End
·START / FINISH·	Grid reference: SW 450241
·DOG FRIENDLINESS·	Dogs on lead through grazed areas
·PARKING·	Lamorna Cove
·PUBLIC TOILETS·	Lamorna Cove

BACKGROUND TO THE WALK

The coast at Lamorna, to the south west of Penzance, is one of the loveliest in Cornwall. This is a south-facing coast, protected from prevailing westerly winds although storms from the south and east can be merciless here, as witnessed by a bitter record of terrible shipwrecks over the years. The bare granite cliffs are enhanced by swathes of lush vegetation that turn the coast into something of a wild garden in spring and summer.

Granite Quarrying

The walk starts from the hugely popular Lamorna Cove, once the scene of granite quarrying. The sturdy quay at Lamorna was built so that ships could load up with the quarried stone, but the swell and the tidal regimen made berthing difficult. Much of the stone was carried overland by horse and wagon to Newlyn Harbour and to Penzance. The coast path west from Lamorna winds its sinuous way through tumbled granite boulders, then climbs steeply to the cliff tops. It passes above Tater du Lighthouse, by jet black, greenstone cliffs, a startling accent in all these miles of golden granite although the upper parts of the greenstone are dusted with ochre-coloured lichen.

Secluded

Soon the path descends steeply to the delightful St Loy's Cove, a secluded boulder beach where a brisk little stream pours out of a wooded valley. Spring comes early at St Loy; the sub-tropical vegetation through which the walk leads reflects the area's mild and moist micro-climate. From St Loy's woods you climb inland to reach two enthralling ancient monuments. The first is the Tregiffian burial chamber, a late Bronze Age entrance grave that was uncovered during road widening in the 1960s. The cup-marked stone is a reproduction, the valuable original is in the County Museum at Truro.

Just along the road from Tregiffian stands one of Cornwall's most famous monuments, the Merry Maidens' stone circle. This Late Neolithic/Bronze Age structure represents an ancient ceremonial and ritual site of major importance. Its popular name, appended by a much later superstitious society, refers to a myth of young girls being turned to stone for dancing on a Sunday. Later in the walk you can see two nearby standing stones, the mythical 'Pipers' who supplied the sacrilegious music. The true spirit of the stones reflects a far more intriguing ancient culture. The final part of the walk leads from the Merry Maidens to a wonderful old trackway that leads over water-worn stones into the Lamorna Valley along a route that may well have originated in the time of the stone circles themselves.

Walk 46 Directions

① From the far end of the seaward car park in the cove, at the end of the terrace above **Lamorna Harbour**, follow the coast path through some short rocky sections. Continue along the coast path past the tops of **Tregurnow Cliff** and **Rosemodress Cliff**.

② Pass above the entrance ramp and steps to **Tater du Lighthouse**. Pass a large residence on the right and then, where the track bends right, keep left along the narrow coast path, at a signpost.

③ Descend steeply (take great care when the ground is muddy) from **Boscawen Cliff** to **St Loy's Cove**. Cross a section of sea-smoothed

Walk 46

boulders that may be slippery when wet. Follow the path inland through dense vegetation and by the stream. Cross a private drive then climb steeply uphill. Go over a stile onto a track, turn right over a stile and follow the path through trees.

④ By a wooden signpost and an old tree, go sharply down right and cross the stream on large boulders, then follow a hedged-in path round left. In about 50yds (46m), by a wooden signpost, go sharp right and up to a surfaced lane. Turn left and follow the lane uphill. At a junction with a bend on another track, keep ahead and uphill. At **Boskenna Farm** buildings follow the surfaced lane round left and keep ahead.

⑤ From the lane, at the entrance drive to a bungalow on the right, the right-of-way goes through a field gate, then cuts across the field corner to a wooden stile in a wire

fence. Beyond this, the way (there's no path) leads diagonally across the field to its top right-hand corner, where a stile leads into a large roadside lay-by with a granite cross at its edge. An alternative to the field route is to continue along the farm lane, and then to turn right along the public road, with care, to reach the lay-by.

⑥ Follow the road to the Tregiffian burial chamber on the right and then to the **Merry Maidens stone circle**. From the stone circle continue to a field corner, then cross over a steep stile. Follow a path diagonally right across the next field towards buildings. Go over a stile onto a road, then go down the left-hand of two lanes, a surfaced lane with a '**No Through Road**' sign.

⑦ Where the lane ends keep ahead onto a public bridleway. Follow a shady and very rocky track downhill to the public road. Turn right and walk down the road, with care, passing the **Lamorna Wink Inn**, to the car park.

The Tinners' Trail at Pendeen

An absorbing walk through the historic tin and copper mining country of the Land's End Peninsula.

•DISTANCE•	5 miles (8km)
•MINIMUM TIME•	4hrs
•ASCENT / GRADIENT•	328ft (100m)
•LEVEL OF DIFFICULTY•	
•PATHS•	Coastal footpath, field paths and moorland tracks
•LANDSCAPE•	Spectacular coastal cliffs, old mining country and open moorland
•SUGGESTED MAP•	aqua3 OS Explorer 102 Land's End
•START / FINISH•	Grid reference: SW 383344
•DOG FRIENDLINESS•	Please keep dogs under control in field sections
•PARKING•	Free car park in centre of Pendeen village, opposite Boscaswell Stores, on the B3306
•PUBLIC TOILETS•	Pendeen car park and Geevor Tin Mine

BACKGROUND TO THE WALK

The tin and copper mines of Pendeen on the north coast of the Land's End Peninsula are redundant, as are all of Cornwall's mines; the culmination of the long decline of Cornish mining since its Victorian heyday. The deep mining of Cornwall lost out to cheap ore from surface strip mines in Asia and to the vagaries of the international market. At Pendeen the area's last working mine of Geevor closed in 1990 after years of uncertainty and false promise and despite vigorous efforts by the local community to save it. Today, the modern buildings of Geevor have been transformed into a fascinating mining museum, but it is the ruined granite chimney stacks and engine houses of the 19th-century industry that have given this mining coast its dramatic visual heritage. Below ground lies the true heritage of hard rock mining.

History and Character

To walk through this post-industrial rural landscape is to walk through a huge slice of Cornish history and character. Early in the walk you reach the Geevor Tin Mine and then the National Trust's Levant Engine House (▶ While You're There). From Levant the coast path runs on to Botallack, where the famous Crown's Mine Engine Houses stand on a spectacular shelf of rock above the Atlantic. The workings of the Crown's Mine ran out for almost 1 mile (1.6km) beneath the sea, and the mine was entered down an angled runway using wagons. You can visit the Crown's Mine Engine Houses by following a series of tracks down towards the sea from the route of the main walk. Flooding was a constant problem for these mines and some of the the earliest ever steam engines were developed to pump water from the workings. On the cliff top above the Crown's Mine the National Trust has restored the 19th-century façade of the Botallack Count House. This was the assaying and administrative centre for all the the surrounding mines.

Walk 47

Moorland Hills

From the Count House the way leads to the old mining villages of Botallack and Carnyorth, before climbing steadily inland to the exhilarating moorland hills of Carnyorth Common. This is the famously haunted landscape of Kenidjack Carn which local superstition identified as the playground of giants and devils. From the high ground the linear pattern of Pendeen's mining coast is spread out before you with the glittering Atlantic beyond. The walk then leads back towards Pendeen and past the Church of St John, built by the mining community in the 1850s from the hand-quarried rock of the hills above, yet another token of the remarkable skills of the Cornish hard rock miner.

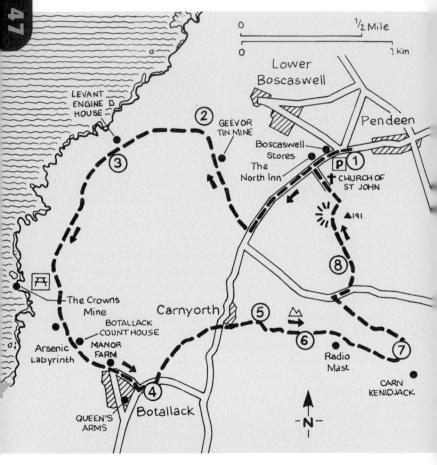

Walk 47 Directions

① Turn left out of the car park and follow the road to the entrance of the **Geevor Tin Mine**. Go down the drive to the reception building and keep to its left down a road between buildings, signposted '**Levant**'.

② Just beyond the buildings, turn left along a narrow path that soon bears right and becomes an unsurfaced track between walls. Turn left at a huge boulder and head towards a very tall chimney stack ahead. Continue across broken ground to the **Levant Engine House**.

WHERE TO EAT AND DRINK ⓘ
Halfway along the route is the **Queen's Arms** in Botallack village, a traditional miners' pub that has retained much of its character. Pub meals are available. The **North Inn** at Pendeen is another traditional inn at the end of the walk and the **Geevor Museum** has a café.

③ Follow the bottom edge of Levant car park and then follow a rough track to reach the **Botallack Count House**. Keep on past **Manor Farm** and reach the public road at **Botallack**. Turn left, the **Queen's Arms** pub is straight down the road ahead.

④ Go left at the main road (watch for fast traffic) then turn left along **Cresswell Terrace** to a stile. Follow field paths to **Carnyorth**. Cross the main road, then follow the lane opposite, turning right at a junction, to reach a solitary house.

⑤ Keep left of the house, go over a stile and cross the field to the opposite hedge to reach a hidden

stile. Follow a path through small fields towards a radio mast. Cross a final stile onto a rough track.

⑥ Go left, then immediately right at a junction. Keep on past the radio mast, then follow a path through gorse and heather to the rocky outcrop of **Carn Kenidjack**, (not always visible when misty).

WHILE YOU'RE THERE ⓘ
A visit to the **Geevor Tin Mine** is worthwhile for the background to the history of Cornish mineral mining. Part of the experience is an underground tour and a visit to the old treatment sheds. The National Trust's restored engine house at **Levant Engine House** contains a remarkable reconstruction of a Cornish beam engine, the great driving force of every Victorian mine. The engine is regularly 'steamed up' to go through the stately rocking motion that powered deep water pumps and facilitated the movement of ore from below ground.

⑦ At a junction abreast of **Carn Kenidjack**, go back left along a path past a small granite parish boundary stone, eventually emerging on a road. Turn right and in about 140yds (128m), go left along an obvious broad track opposite a house.

⑧ Keep left at a junction. By two large stones on the left, bear off right along a grassy track. Go left over a big stone stile directly above the church and descend to the main road. Turn right to the **car park**.

WHAT TO LOOK FOR ⓘ
Just below the track that runs past the Botallack Count House lie the ruins of an **arsenic labyrinth**. Mineral ore was often contaminated with arsenic. In the 19th century during times of low tin prices, this arsenic was collected by roasting ore in a calciner and passing the smoke through enclosed tunnels, the labyrinth. The cooling vapour deposited the arsenic on the labyrinth walls as a powder that was then exported, mainly to America as a pesticide against the boll weevil in the cotton fields. Its effect on both the labyrinth workers and cotton pickers does not bear thinking about.

Golden Beaches and Cliffs at Porthcurno

Along interlocking footpaths between sandy coves and granite cliffs on the Land's End Peninsula.

•DISTANCE•	3½ miles (5.7km)
•MINIMUM TIME•	2hrs 30min
•ASCENT / GRADIENT•	164ft (50m) ▲▲ ▲▲ ▲
•LEVEL OF DIFFICULTY•	🚶 🚶 🚶
•PATHS•	Coastal footpath
•LANDSCAPE•	Granite sea cliffs and inland heath
•SUGGESTED MAP•	aqua3 OS Explorer 107 St Austell & Liskeard
•START / FINISH•	Grid reference: SW 384224
•DOG FRIENDLINESS•	Dogs should be kept under control on beaches
•PARKING•	Porthcurno, St Levan and Porthgwarra
•PUBLIC TOILETS•	Porthgwarra and Porthleven

BACKGROUND TO THE WALK

Land's End may be the ultimate visitor destination in Cornwall (▶ Walk 50). It is the most westerly point certainly and its cliffs are nothing less than spectacular; but for the true aficionado of coastal scenery, the granite cliffs of Porthcurno and Porthgwarra, to the south of Land's End, are hard to beat for their beauty and sculpted form. The area has even more esoteric distinction. Gwennap Head, at Porthgwarra, is the most southerly point on the Land's End Peninsula. The Atlantic tidal flow divides at the base of Gwennap's spectacular Chair Ladder cliff, one flow running eastwards up the English Channel, the other running north, up St George's Channel between Britain and Ireland. Partly because of this, Gwennap Head is sometimes known as 'the Fishermen's Land's End', a title that rather puts the other Land's End in its place.

Golden Sand

This walk starts at Porthcurno, where a sweeping expanse of almost white shell sand lies at the heart of an arc of golden granite cliffs that embrace the small bay. On the south side lies the rocky coxcomb of Treryn Dinas, or Logan Rock. To the north is the famous Minack Open Air Theatre, built within the rocky ribs of the headland. The final section of the walk passes the Minack, but first the route leads inland and across fields to the splendid little Church of St Levan, couched in one of the few sheltered spots on this robust coast. Below the church a shallow valley runs down to Chapel Porth Beach, more besieged by tides than Porthcurno, but still a delightful place, especially in summer. Again the beach here is left for later in the walk, whose route now leads along the coast path and then climbs inland before dropping down to Porthgwarra Cove, where tunnels and caverns in the cliff were carved out by farmers and fishermen to give better access to the narrow beach. From Porthgwarra, you head back along the coast path to Porth Chapel, (for a visit to Gwennap Head, ▶ Walk 49). The path leads you down past the little Well of St Levan. Below here there is a rocky access path to the beach.

Spectacular Steps

The route of the walk leads steeply up to Rospletha Point and then to the remarkable cliff face theatre at Minack (➤ What to Look For). From here, the most direct way down to Porthcurno Beach is by a series of very steep steps that may not suit everyone. But if you don't mind the vertiginous experience, the views really are outstanding. You can avoid this descent by some judicious road walking. Either way Porthcurno's glorious beach is at hand in the cove below you.

Walk 48 Directions

① From the car park, walk back up the approach road, then just beyond the **Porthcurno Hotel**, turn sharply left along a track and follow it to reach cottages. Pass to the right of the cottages and go through a metal kissing gate. Follow a field path past a granite cross.

② Enter **St Levan** churchyard by a granite stile. Go round the far side of the church to the entrance gate and onto a surfaced lane. Cross the lane and follow the path opposite, signposted '**Porthgwarra Cove**'. Cross a footbridge over a stream then in about 55yds (50m), at a junction, take the right fork and follow the path to merge with the main coast path and keep ahead.

Walk 48

③ Just after the path begins to descend towards **Porthgwarra Cove,** branch off right up some wooden steps. Reach a track and turn up right, then at a road, turn left.

④ Go round a sharp left-hand bend, then at a footpath signpost, go right down a grassy path and cross a stone footbridge. Continue uphill to reach a bend on a track, just up from large granite houses.

WHERE TO EAT AND DRINK ⓘ

There is a seasonal café at **Porthgwarra**, ideally located at the midway point in the walk. Porthcurno has several outlets including the **Beach Café** and the **Cable Inn**. A seasonal ice cream and soft drinks van is usually located in the Porthcurno car park.

---

⑤ Turn left, go over a stile beside a gate, then continue down a surfaced lane to **Porthgwarra Cove.** Opposite the shop and café, go right down a track, signposted '**Coast Path**' then follow the path round left in front of a house. Go sharp right at a junction and climb steps.

⑥ Continue along the coast path, partly reversing the previous route past Point ④. Keep right at junctions, and eventually descend past **St Levan's Well** to just above

---

WHILE YOU'RE THERE ⓘ

The **Museum of Submarine Telegraphy** at Porthcurno, located above the top end of the car park, rewards a visit. It records the long history of undersea cable telegraphy. In its time, Porthcurno was the world's largest international cable station. The museum is contained within underground tunnels that served as a secret communications base during the Second World War.

Porth Chapel Beach. (Dogs should be kept under control on the beach.) Follow the coast path steeply over **Pedn-mên-an-mere**, and continue to the car park of the **Minack Theatre** (► What to Look For).

⑦ For the surefooted, cross the car park and go down the track to the left of the **Minack** compound, then descend the steep and dramatic cliff steps, with great care. When the path levels off, continue to a junction. The right fork takes you to **Porthcurno Beach** and back to the car park. The continuation leads to the road opposite the **Beach Café**, where a right turn leads to the car park. A less challenging alternative to the cliff steps is to turn left out of the Minack car park. Follow the approach road to a T-junction with a public road. Turn right and walk down the road, watching out for traffic.

WHAT TO LOOK FOR ⓘ

The **Minack Theatre** was the unusual creation of Rowena Cade, whose family bought the rocky headland above Porthcurno Beach in the 1920s. A general interest in theatre led to the staging of Shakespeare's *The Tempest* on a makeshift stage on the cliffs in 1932. Miss Cade, ably assisted by skilled local gardeners and builders then developed the Minack over many years into a full scale theatre, carved out of the cliffs, a Cornish version in miniature of the great classical theatres of Greece and Rome, but with a stupendous backdrop. Today atmospheric performances of a variety of plays and musicals are staged during the summer months. A Minack performance is an unbeatable experience. Wine and light clothes for balmy summer evenings; full scale waterproofs and hot chocolate otherwise.

Gwennap Head and Porthgwarra Cove

A short extension to Walk 48 takes you across 'the Fishermen's Land's End'.
See map and information panel for Walk 48

•DISTANCE•	2 miles (3.2km) for this extra loop
•MINIMUM TIME•	1hr
•ASCENT / GRADIENT•	164ft (50m) ▲▲ ▲ ▲
•LEVEL OF DIFFICULTY•	林 林 林

Walk 49 Directions
(Walk 48 option)

You can extend the main walk by following the coast path across **Gwennap Head** to the west of **Porthgwarra Cove**. At Point ⑤ on the main walk turn right onto the rough track, then, at the left-hand bend, go off right along a grassy track. In 30yds (27m), where the track forks, take the right fork and follow a grassy track across the open heathland, a glorious mosaic of purple heather and golden gorse in late summer. Keep left at the next fork and soon pass through a gap in a lichened granite wall. A few paces beyond the wall, take the left fork at a junction of tracks. Keep ahead along the track to reach the coast path, Point Ⓐ, by an old tyre capstan, once used as part of a moving target line for military rifle training. Turn left here along a short path and in a few steps merge with the main coast path abreast of a big lichen-covered rock.

Go through the granite wall ahead and at a fork keep left and descend gently to the bend in the track by Point ⑤ once more. Turn right up the track, then, in about 30yds (27m), turn off right up a narrow path that leads to the **National Coastwatch lookout**, where you turn left along the coast path. Follow the path past two incongruous, brightly painted concrete cones, Point Ⓑ, protruding from the heather. These are not Cornish missiles that failed to make it out of their silos. They are landmarks to assist mariners in fixing the position of the dangerous **Runnelstone Reef**, also marked offshore by a buoy whose wind-activated siren can often be heard moaning eerily. Follow the coast path all the way round **Hella Point** to reach the surfaced road above **Porthgwarra Cove** where you re-join Walk 48 at Point ⑤.

WHAT TO LOOK FOR ⓘ

In spring daffodils line the cliff path on the approach to Porthgwarra from St Levan. Later in the year the heathland behind Gwennap Head is a mosaic of purple heather and ling and golden gorse. This area is also famed as a stopping off place for migrant birds, especially in autumn, when some very rare species, such as the American red-eyed vireo, (*Vireo olivaceous*), are often blown off course all the way across the Atlantic to this landfall of Europe.

The Scenic Route from St Just to Land's End

Walking the far western coast of Cornwall to the 'First and Last' edge of England.

•DISTANCE•	6½ miles (10.4km)
•MINIMUM TIME•	3hrs 30min
•ASCENT / GRADIENT•	328ft (100m) ▲▲▲
•LEVEL OF DIFFICULTY•	徒 徒 徒
•PATHS•	Good coastal footpaths. Can be rocky in places
•LANDSCAPE•	West-facing coast with low cliffs and golden beach
•SUGGESTED MAP•	aqua3 OS Explorer 102 Land's End
•START•	Grid reference: SW 369314
•FINISH•	Grid reference: SW 344250
•DOG FRIENDLINESS•	Dogs on lead through grazed areas. Notices indicate
•PARKING•	St Just main car park on Market Street, opposite St Just Library. Large free car park
•PUBLIC TOILETS•	St Just free car park, Sennen, Land's End
•NOTE•	The No 15 service bus runs between Land's End and St Just. Four buses each way weekdays, six on Sundays

Walk 50 Directions

Most people reach Land's End by car and must first run the persuasive gauntlet of the commercial 'Land's End Experience', a welcoming party of themed exhibitions that lies between car park and cliff edge. The real Land's End experience is overpowering, of course. Towering granite cliffs rise up from an always restless sea. This savage headland was *Belerion* to the Romans, the 'Seat of Storms', a murderous place for sailing vessels caught against its unforgiving coastline. Offshore lies the Longships Lighthouse on its sliver of rock. Far to the south west, on clear days, you can pick out the tiny profiles of the Isles of Scilly. Beyond all this is the Atlantic, and then America.

Land's End is spectacular enough, but leading away to either side of the headland are the long corrugated north and south coastlines of the ever-widening Penwith Peninsula, coastlines that often outclass Land's End for drama and beauty. By way of taking the long view towards Land's End this walk follows footpaths from the old

> **WHILE YOU'RE THERE** ⓘ
>
> **St Just** was once at the heart of Cornish coastal mining and is an attractive town to explore. Its central square is surrounded by shops and a number of pubs and is flanked at one corner by a handsome granite church with 15th-century features. Around the church are several fine old cottages and buildings. As a major centre of Methodism St Just also has an imposing Wesleyan church from 1833, that once served a congregation of over 2,000.

The section of coast from Porth Nanven to Aire Point has some remarkable examples of raised beach. These are sections of wave-cut platforms that are now above sea level. Their exposed surfaces are peppered with sea-polished boulders and pebbles. The phenomenon is the result of an upward tilting of Northern Europe after the ice caps melted during the post glacial period, thus easing pressure on the land mass. The finest example of a raised beach is the seaward cliff face on the north side of Porth Nanven. Don't go too close to raised beaches as they are usually unstable.

mining town of St Just and then along an exhilarating stretch of coast that runs south to Sennen Cove and to Land's End and faces due west into the bracing Atlantic.

You start at **St Just's Market Square** and go down **Market Street**, to the right of the **Commercial Hotel**, and past the free car park and **Library**. At a T-junction, turn left and follow **Bosorne Terrace**, keeping straight ahead at a junction by a memorial park. Where the road curves left at another junction, keep right and follow a lane signposted '**Unsuitable for Motors**.' After ¼ mile (400m) the lane ends by a seat. Go right from here and follow a hedged-in track. At a junction go left and downhill past **Brook Cottage**, then turn right down stone steps and follow an enclosed path across a stream to reach a junction with a track. Turn right here, then left onto a lane that leads down a narrow valley to the sea.

This is **Cot Valley**, a sheltered enclave on an otherwise bare and windswept coast. As always in the St Just area, this landscape was heavily mined for copper and tin from as early as Tudor times. From the mouth of the valley, at **Porth Nanven**, you cross the stream and follow the coast path uphill. To the left of the coast path are the gaping vents of old mining 'adits', tunnels into the cliff face created by early miners excavating veins of rich ore. It is dangerous to enter these adits. Offshore lie the rocky islands of the Brisons, said to have once served as a castaway prison for criminals. For the next few miles (km) the path picks a delightful way past boulder-crammed beaches and above crumbling cliffs, then descends almost to sea level. Soon you are on the the great surfing beaches of **Gwynver** and **Sennen.** Here the Atlantic swells race in across a vast expanse of clean, flat sand and the air positively fizzes with ozone. At **Sennen Cove** follow the seafront walkway to reach the lifeboat house and the **Round House Gallery**, a circular wooden building that once contained a huge capstan used to haul fishing boats onto dry land. Beyond here, go through the car park then climb steadily uphill to the rocky headland of **Pedn-Men-Du**, where the National Trust has a seasonal information centre. From here the coastal footpath follows the edge of the cliffs to the 'First and Last' headland in England and to the relentless celebration of the **Land's End Experience**.

Walking in Safety

All these walks are suitable for any reasonably fit person, but less experienced walkers should try the easier walks first. Route finding is usually straightforward, but you will find that an Ordnance Survey map is a useful addition to the route maps and descriptions.

Risks

Although each walk here has been researched with a view to minimising the risks to the walkers who follow its route, no walk in the countryside can be considered to be completely free from risk. Walking in the outdoors will always require a degree of common sense and judgement to ensure that it is as safe as possible.

- Be particularly careful on cliff paths and in upland terrain, where the consequences of a slip can be very serious.

- Remember to check tidal conditions before walking on the seashore.

- Some sections of route are by, or cross, busy roads. Take care and remember traffic is a danger even on minor country lanes.

- Be careful around farmyard machinery and livestock, especially if you have children with you.

- Be aware of the consequences of changes in the weather and check the forecast before you set out. Carry spare clothing and a torch if you are walking in the winter months. Remember the weather can change very quickly at any time of the year, and in moorland and heathland areas, mist and fog can make route finding much harder. Don't set out in these conditions unless you are confident of your navigation skills in poor visibility. In summer remember to take account of the heat and sun; wear a hat and carry spare water.

- On walks away from centres of population you should carry a whistle and survival bag. If you do have an accident requiring the emergency services, make a note of your position as accurately as possible and dial 999.

Acknowledgements

Des Hannigan would like to thank the National Trust for Cornwall, and Cornwall County Council for advice and guidance during his research for this book. A very special thank you to Mike Rasdall and Stella White, and to David and Sally Hillebrandt for their kind help and hospitality. The greatest acknowledgement must go to all those agencies, landholders and individuals who do so much professional and voluntary work in maintaining Cornwall's invaluable network of footpaths and tracks.

Series management: Outcrop Publishing Services, Cumbria
Series editor: Chris Bagshaw
Front cover: AA Photo Library/P Goodrum